ACHIEVING LARGE

GOALS

Keith Dahlberg
Dad

1

Also by Keith Dahlberg:

Edwin T. Dahlberg   Pastor, Peacemaker, Prophet

Flame Tree   A Novel of Modern Burma

Bridge Ahead   A Medical Memoir

Access to Medical Care

The Samana Incident

South Sea Gold

Achieving Large

Goals

True Stories of Accomplishment

By Keith Dahlberg

Copyright © 2015 by Keith R. Dahlberg

All rights reserved.

This is a work of non-fiction about real people, most of them still living. I have consulted the principal individuals in each chapter, and they have consented to have their stories published. It is not my intent to interfere with those who are themselves writing to publish.

ISBN - 13: 978-1517459451

ISBN – 10: 1517459451

Printed in the United States (date) by CreateSpace

TABLE OF CONTENTS

ACKNOWLEDGEMENTS

I am indebted to each of the people in this book who have given me a window on their work, their lives and hopes.

My thanks to those who have patiently given technical support to my writing in this unfamiliar age of computers: Diana Johns, Chris Hohns, and the staff of The Mouse Pad computer shop in Pinehurst, Idaho: Rick Fuller, Ben Nesler, and Brittany Brower.

Thanks also to the Silver Valley Writers Group and it's aspiring authors and editors, and to my niece, Joan Magill and her husband Tom, for their knowledge of clinical psychology and business; to my son-in-law Cleve Ashcraft for his mathematics expertise, and for the many other cheerleaders among friends and family who have encouraged me to keep on writing.

And most especially, my love and thanks to my wife Lois, our children Sue, Pat, John, Nancy, and our grandchildren, for all their support.

About the cover. Thanks to Rikki Rogers Graphic Design, in Marion, Illinois, who has done the eye-catching covers for both South Sea Gold and Achieving Large Goals.

PREFACE

The stories in this book are about people I have met, people whose lives have had a favorable influence on people or the conditions around them. Some were single-day encounters, others were my colleagues for years. Some exhibit noticeable faults as we all do at times, yet they were different from the crowd, different enough to prompt me to look more deeply into their lives.

This is not a handbook for sales people or business executives, as the title might suggest, although I hope that they will be among those who find these stories intriguing. Nor have I much interest in doctrinal interpretations, or promoting any political viewpoint. After fifty years of medical/surgical practice, along with nineteen as an author of fiction and non-fiction, I see people as interesting stories, some with remarkable outcomes. I have special interest in the physical sciences, religion, linguistics, travel, writing, and history.

These chapters are presented in no particular order, except to begin with several honest and competent people having effect mostly in their own community. They tend to do what many of us consider "the right thing" when presented with a chance to help someone else. Perhaps their parents raised them to do that; perhaps it was just pride in doing their job well, a sense of satisfaction that grows with repeated performance. In any case, this is what they often do.

The chapters move on to a second group, similar except that these have had an opportunity to make a widespread difference in the world or in a large region of it, and they have achieved that difference. They may never have foreseen the result or even conceived of it. But it did happen. Call it chance, call it "the right time", heroic effort, or whatever else you choose, but in the end it has turned out very well. Our finite brains may not be able to see for certain why, but we can speculate later.

In a third group, I note a coincidence of factors in each case, that lead me to suspect that something beyond blind chance or personal effort is at work in those people's lives.

A word about the way I write: in conversations with people of different backgrounds, we are all exposed to expressions that might not seem appropriate in polite society. I usually avoid using a few terms I have heard in the mines or in medical school. But occasionally a coarse word helps portray someone's character in a manner that no paragraph of explanation would do. I mean no disrespect to any individual in my reporting someone's manner of speech.

Keith Dahlberg   October, 2015

.

Chapter 1

ARNOLD: MASTER BUILDER

Arnold, with my wife and I, had just finished inspecting our back yard where the new garage would go. He had my sketched floor plan in his hand, and had changed the dimensions enough to allow space for a couple of pickup trucks, this being Idaho where a gun-rack in the rear window is important for everyone except those few of us who prefer forty miles to the gallon more than two elk in the back.

His weather-tanned face concentrated on the sketch for about a minute, and then, "Okay, I'll get the permits Monday and we'll get Ron's backhoe in here and start work the next day."

"So, how much advance do you need for materials and all?" I asked.

"By golly, I don't do business that way. You can pay me when the job is done." His tone allowed no argument. And that was it. No written contract. I knew Arnold and he knew me. No blueprints either. The sketch he had marked up would be enough for the County Building Inspectors; they knew Arnold's work too, although they always checked the concrete and rebar for the foundation, and other items as the work progressed. In the twenty-five years since he had immigrated from Central Europe, Arnold had become something of a local institution, and soon had a reputation for honesty and competent work.

He arrived in the USA at age twenty-four, speaking mostly German, leaving his brother and five sisters in Switzerland. He came to Idaho where a man he knew was logging around Priest Lake. Back in the Alps of Europe, Arnold had run a skyline for him— the mile-long rope that hauls logs off the slopes—and he was soon working for the man again. Later he moved to Idaho's Silver Valley as a carpenter and builder. And to ski.

Always ready for a beer or a cigaret after work was done for the day, he might also be found up on stage at some local event, pumping out a polka on his accordion, or just enjoying the crowd. The phone message on his answering machine never changed: "I'm not here right now, but leave a message and I'll get back atcha."

Arnold wasted no time starting a job. When my old garage was leaning over like the Tower of Pisa, he appeared with his crew and backhoe at 1:30 p.m. Within an hour they had the building down and scraped into a neat pile. They carefully watched the pile of debris burn until 5:00 p.m., then left it to a watchman with a water hose. Although they had scraped all the tar paper off the roof boards before torching the pile, in accordance with the fire chief's regulations, I noticed that the pile of tar paper was a little smaller each time I looked out the window, as Arnold chucked a piece or two into the fire, until he only had enough debris left to fill the back of his pickup. Arnold is practical above all else.

But on any job, he always had time to talk a bit over a cup of coffee in our kitchen before getting down to business. We learned we both had ancestors in Bern, Switzerland. We shared reminiscences of housing problems we each had when moving into the Silver Valley. I recall the time he spotted a mango sitting on my window sill—it being new to him, he wanted to know all about it, "but won't try one now —got to get to work." After a quick comment on the hummingbird at the feeder by the back door, he is "back at it" with his surveyor scope and string line, or hammering planks into forms for when the concrete truck will arrive.

Now in 2015 twenty years later, the two-car garage with its cement floor and ramp, and metal roof and siding over sturdy wooden frame, and remotely controlled doors, is still as good as new, still with plenty of room to spare "in case the next owner has a camper," as Arnold explained.

Arnold and his one-man assistant (and a dog) later added a downstairs bedroom, bath and utility room to our house in 2007. Same excellent work; subcontracting the plumbing and electric wiring. The final bill, in each case has been detailed, supported by receipts for all materials and, in my opinion, very reasonably priced.

He is retired, after several work injuries from over the years. He once dislocated a shoulder that somehow tore the main artery to his right arm and would have killed him before the Medivac helicopter even arrived if the pressure of surrounding muscles had not confined the blood loss. No longer permitted to raise his arm above shoulder level forced him to stop any construction work where he would have to hammer nails above his head. But at age 79, he is still only semi-retired; last summer he cut forty cords of firewood. When I asked how he could load a cord of wood into his pickup, he confided that he had a step-up that allowed him to climb high enough to load it without raising his arm.

Over cups of coffee last March, as we compared our ages, he demanded to know my birth date. I don't usually reveal the day, and asked him why he needed to know.

"Because I'm going to phone you that morning, and play Happy Birthday on my accordion!"

O-o-kay . . . I will always remember him with respect and affection as a competent and honest builder, and friend.

Chapter 2

THE UTAH AUTO MECHANIC

After graduating from medical school in Syracuse, I did my year of rotating internship at Denver's Presbyterian Hospital: three months each on Obsterics, Internal Medicine, Pediatrics, and General Surgery. At the end of that year, two interns applied for the surgical resident position. The other one, Bob Linnemeyer was chosen, but the hospital also wanted me to stay on. "We are beginning a new residency program in obstetrics and gynecology," the hospital director told me. "If you want to spend a year on that, you can go on to the following year's opening in surgery."

That was ideal for me; I had already signed up for overseas mission work and knew I would need training in both fields. So I delivered babies and did pelvic surgery for a year, starting in July 1955, and then moved on to general surgery in mid-1956.

The hospital ran a prenatal clinic in the Hispanic

part of Denver, which provided me with about thirty baby deliveries each month. The staff surgeons supervised my hysterectomies and Caesarian sections, and let me take out an occasional appendix. I learned to manage pregnancy in leukemia, pregnancy in advanced cancer, pregnancy in toxemia, severe allergy, heart disease and many other complications. Abortion was still strictly illegal, and there were many victims of whatever method neighbors gossiped about over backyard fences. That year, women with severe hemorrhage were common. During exam of such patients I would often find a round ulcer on the uterine cervix, briskly bleeding from a damaged artery. "You put in a purple pill (potassium permanganate) didn't you," I'd say.

"How did you know!" she would ask.

"Don't ever use it again. It's dangerous. There are safe ways to prevent getting pregnant if you don't want another baby."

But for all I learned in the OB/GYN residency, some of the best lessons came from outside the hospital's program. Lois and I took a few days vacation during Thanksgiving that year to explore westward. We put one-year-old Susie and her crib in the back seat of our old Plymouth, and set out over Loveland Pass on Highway 6 with Salt Lake City as our goal. Neither of us had ever been as far as Utah. We stayed overnight at Grand Junction, toured the misty crags and spires of Colorado National Monument next morning, and drove across the sagebrush-covered Utah desert. We stopped to buy gas at the town of Price, before heading up over the pass called Soldier's Summit.

The sky darkened, wet snow began falling. The road soon had slippery snow three-inches deep. The windshield wiper on the old car worked poorly at best, and now I had to stick my head out the open window to see where I was going. Ahead of us, a highway truck dropped cinders on the road, and I tried to steer in his tracks. Still headed uphill, we had no idea how far we had to go to get to the top.

The engine sputtered, died, then caught again. This happened several times, allowing the cinder truck to pull far ahead of us in the blinding snow. The car began to skid; other cars and trucks honked as they pulled around us. Susie, although warm enough in her snowsuit, was hungry and we had no way to warm a bottle. Not liking the cold milk, she began to cry. Lois held her on her lap, singing a lullaby. Our progress became slower and slower; snow blurred my glasses when my head was out the window. Maximum stress. "Can't we have a little quiet in here till we get to the top!" I finally snarled.

The engine gave one last cough, and died for good. I coasted to the shoulder of the road and tried the starter several times. It didn't catch. I got out, raised the hood, stared at the engine as snowflakes hissed on its hot rusty metal. Lois looked frightened; I felt the same way. Without the engine, the car's heater grew cold. It was dark now, and we were miles from anywhere.

About fifteen minutes later, a large car pulled over, a Buick maybe, or a Lincoln. The driver offered us a lift; we thankfully retrieved the diaper bag and one suitcase; locked our car and climbed into the warmth of our rescuer's back seat. I don't know what he thought of two young kids and a baby out in the snow, but he took us over the pass, down to the tiny town of Thistle, and let us off at the only motel. I found a tow-truck number, phoned, and rode with the driver to our car. The mechanic said it was probably the timer, and towed it to his garage until morning.

Next day, with a new timer and a towing bill receipt that had taken half of our cash, we were on our way again. Soon the engine sputtered and died. We talked about just heading home, but the towns lay ahead of us, and a hundred miles of desert behind. I pulled into a garage in Provo. "It keeps sputtering and dying," I said.

He raised the hood. "When did you last get new spark plugs?"

"I dunno. Not in the two years we've had it."

"That's probably it, then." He put in new plugs, charged us six dollars, and we headed toward Salt Lake. Our money supply was almost gone. The engine kept on skipping; we nursed it along until Salt Lake City, and headed into another garage.

"This is the third garage today," I told the gray-haired mechanic. "If you can't fix it, we'll give you the car for enough bus fare to get us back to Denver."

"Well, tell me just how it behaves," he said. I described in detail what had been going on since we had refueled at Price the day before. He listened, asked several questions, then told me, "You don't need to sell your car." He handed me a can . "Pour this in your gas tank. It'll take the water and ice out of your fuel line." He charged us fifty cents. We had no further trouble the entire five hundred miles back to Denver.

That third auto mechanic taught me how to question a patient, a lesson I've carried through my whole professional life: Don't assume a diagnosis. Listen to the patient's story first. Medical school taught me the right questions to ask. The garage mechanic taught me to listen to the answers.

Chapter 3

ED, MASTER PLUMBER

I'll tell you what, Doc," Ed said as he surveyed my failed attempt to repair the faucet on my kitchen sink, "I won't try to take out anybody's tonsils, if you'll promise to leave the plumbing alone." Over the years, each of us has respected the other's abilities in our chosen fields. Each knew when the other was in trouble, and would be promptly available, be it severe illness or a frozen water pipe.

A couple of years after I opened my new office in Pinehurst, the office toilet unaccountably started overflowing. Beyond trying the plunger—unsuccessfully—I remembered my promise, and called Ed.

"Well," Ed reported after his first inspection, "you've got that 4-inch vent pipe out in the bushes beyond the back parking lot. The cover's off, and I wonder if some kids in the neighborhood have been rolling rocks down it and plugged your drain." We negotiated a price for this major surgery on the parking lot. If the blockage was beyond the junction with the main sewer line, the sewer district would pay for it.

"But I kind of think it's in your branch line," he mused.

"Well, okay, go ahead and see," I said.

My main memory of that afternoon is of a tremendous hole twelve feet deep, with Ed and his cane balancing on top of a mound of dirt and pavement slabs at its edge. A chugging sump pump spewed a stream of groundwater out onto the parking lot. His two sons in the pit below us scrambled for dry ground as the opened drain pipe from the depths disgorged a three-feet-long, four-inch diameter plug, followed by the pent-up collection of about a week's waste.

Ed leaned on his cane and voiced satisfaction with his correct diagnosis. Ever the philosopher, he added, "I always tell my boys, 'Don't be afraid of that stuff; all of it was good enough at one time for somebody to eat.'"

To the best of my knowledge, Ed's was the only family I treated through five generations. His mother was a patient of mine in the nursing home, and even past the age of ninety she wanted to be sure each year when New Year's Eve came round, that I remembered to tell the nurses it was okay for her to join the family at home for the evening. And for the fifth generation, I delivered Ed's granddaughter's baby boy.

Ed and his mother are both gone now, but his practical advice still lives on. When his daughter-in-law came in for a checkup one day, I asked her what her son was doing now that he was out of the army.

"Oh, he's apprenticed to Dad in the plumbing business." She thought a moment and giggled. "The first night, he came home from work and said Grandpa had told him three things that a plumber has to memorize:

Payday is Friday.

Shit don't run up-hill, and

Don't bite your fingernails."

Chapter 4

JOHN T. CLOUGH: MINISTER OF MUSIC

John Clough (rhymes with cuff), his wife and small son lived in an apartment on the roof of the church, seven stories above the streets of downtown Syracuse, NY.

First Baptist Church of Syracuse was arguably the only church in America that operated a major hotel, restaurant, and 2,000-member church all in one building simultaneously and successfully.

The Cloughs were full-time directors of the church's six choirs. Together with organist George Oplinger, they provided superior music on Sundays and occasional public concerts, plus voice lessons in cases where a choir's performance would benefit.

We high school and college students in the youth choir sang, not out of a sense of duty but because singing was a pleasure and we knew we sounded good. Mr. Clough allowed informality and occasional horseplay, but he knew how to maintain discipline and get the best from our combined voices. He conducted without waving his arms, but kept our attention focused on slight motions of his wrists and hands.

In 1944, the Northern Baptist Churches established a national conference grounds at Green Lake, Wisconsin, which offered a variety of Christian conferences during the summer season. The executive director, Dr. Luther Wesley Smith, asked Mr. Clough to take charge of the music during the second summer season. He agreed, and because he wanted to have at least a few of us from Syracuse who were already familiar with his style, he began talking up the new eleven-hundred-acre estate on the shores of Green Lake among us in Syracuse. He convinced several adults and three of us high school students to apply for work on the staff. That summer, as soon as school let out we three boys, Chuck Perrine, Ed Boyd, and myself, went by train to Fond du Lac, Wisconsin, then transferred to the two-car train to Green Lake, 30 miles west.

With World War II just winding down, youths 18 and older were unavailable, so we 16 and 17 year-olds worked in the dining room, the kitchen, on the waterfront and the hotel lobby. The pay was low, but food, lodging, tips, and all conferences and grounds facilities were free. The 70 student staffers, the 500 delegates of the one-week youth conference, and the one-week recreation workshop, provided a large pool of guys and girls from all over the USA and beyond.

Many, I discovered, had about the same interests and world outlook as my own.

That summer changed my life.

Not all of the conferences interested me, but on many evenings speakers opened my eyes to life and work in other countries. I already had decided that church work was not my thing; chemistry, rocks and minerals fascinated me. One of the guys on the staff introduced me to hitch-hiking on our days off, and I was soon finding mineral specimens from Wisconsin to add to my collection back home. But more than that, I found that there were many kinds of Christian work other than just going to church.

It would be another year before I found my calling in medical missions, but the seed had been planted that summer I was sixteen.

If it had not been for John Clough, and a series of new ideas that arose from his guiding me into work at Green Lake, I might never have become a doctor. I returned to work for five more summers—in 1953, the last one, with my bride, who became camp nurse while I worked as a bus driver.

During those years, several others at Syracuse FBC spent summers on the Green Lake staff in Wisconsin. At least five entered foreign missions, including Syracuse University's football quarterback, and five more entered full-time ministry in USA. And I have met quite a few workers on foreign mission fields in later years who had been on the staff at Green Lake.

Mr. Clough continued in Syracuse for several years beyond my time at medical school; the last I knew, a 1958 news clipping reported him leading a large choir at the New York State Fair, gathered from fifty central New York churches, and featuring a program of Catholic, Protestant and Jewish music traditions. His music has inspired many.

Chapter 5

FREDERICA SMITH: HIGH SCHOOL TEACHER

During my senior year in high school, there were two teachers devoted to teaching English. Miss Bush was a sturdy middle-aged former athlete, known for her no nonsense approach to the curriculum, and her habit of pulling her large desk up to her chair rather than the other way around. The other, Miss Frederica Smith, whose class it was my good fortune to be in, wore horn-rimmed spectacles and had an independent and imaginative approach to education.

Miss Smith sent an article to New York State Education, entitled "Verse Making Is Fun". I take the liberty of quoting from it, sixty-nine years later. She, having passed on to her reward, is no longer available to give permission. Her published article read as follows:

The senior English class had been studying poetry and verse making for less than two weeks when the teacher, Miss Frederica Smith, remarked casually,

"Tomorrow is Valentine's Day, the perfect time to put your new skills to work; for, of course, you all realize that we never take up your time in teaching you vain nothings . . . and everybody should be able to turn out a good Valentine."

The class groaned.

"Oh, my dear brethren and sisters," continued the teacher, in what she hoped sounded like the saccharine voice of the crocodile in How the Elephant Got His Trunk, "You haven't heard the half of it yet."

The class groaned harder, but sat up with increased interest.

"You will choose some character from the literature you have indulged in for the past four years, and write an appropriate Valentine to him—or her."

At once the clamor of genuine interest rose. There was a rapid-fire questioning and answering for three or four minutes. The last question came from the Baptist minister's son. "Is the Bible considered literature?" And we decided that it certainly was.

The next day all but one student out of fifty-seven appeared, verses in hand. Of course they were comparing their masterpieces before they came to the classroom; they were so obviously enjoying the fun that we turned the class into a committee of the whole and enjoyed the Valentines together. Fifteen or twenty were really passably fair. Everyone showed a consciousness of versification. The class selected the following three as worthy of sending to New York State Education:

The first one was written by Marcia Coons, subsequently salutatorian of her class and a winner of a state scholarship.

A MESSAGE TO MRS. MICAWBER ON THE ANNIVERSARY OF ST. VALENTINE'S DAY FROM HER LOVING HUSBAND, T. H. MICAWBER, ESQUIRE

Though Fortune at present is frowning on me

And we shall have nothing but biscuits for tea,

I've ten plans in my head—every one is a pip;

And with you standing by me, there won't be a slip.

Our marriage has borne every blow from the start,

Yet our love for each other will never depart.

Let us look to the day when joy fills our cup,

For, SOMETHING, my darling, WILL SURELY TURN UP.

The next poem was written by Keith Dahlberg, the aforementioned son of a local minister, and also a subsequent winner of a state scholarship.

TO THE QUEEN OF SHEBA

(Note to secretary: File the original under "general correspondence" and make 1,000 copies.

Solomon)

> At this time of the year, ere the first hint of
>   Spring,
> Love's glow passes over not even the king.
> Alas, I am smitten and forced to confess
> That you are essential to life's happiness.
>
>
> In the judging of feminine sweet pulchritude
> It's conceded by all that I've great aptitude.
> I've searched many nations and crossed the
>   Great Sea,
> But never have found the near equal of thee.
>
>
> Of castles and lands I've full many a score;
> Of sapphires and rubies possess I yet more.
> But all of these treasurers I cherish as mine
> I would gladly relinquish for *you* Valentine.

The delight of the audience can easily be imagined [Miss Smith continued.] The perpetrator, however, did not bow and take his seat; instead he said with a face utterly devoid of expression, "I have another."

"Which certainly must be read to be appreciated," rejoined the teacher, balancing precariously on her chair. And then there followed:

POSTSCRIPT TO DELILAH

(See the story of Samson in the book of Judges):

In the course of your making my people feel blue,

Though I'm fighting with thousands, yet think I of you.

I've torn city gates from their place in the wall,

But your icy cold heart I cannot move at all.

In times of distress I've relied on my brawn,

But that's no help at all when to you I am drawn.

Of all the Philistines I think you're most fair,

But, Baby, I can't keep you out of my hair!

They say that the shouts of laughter rocked the girders supporting the school walls.

I didn't appreciate English class greatly at the time, but Miss Smith's class made a difference in my self-confidence. Until then, albeit not exactly a misfit, I was certainly not part of the "In Group". I felt like a total loss at physical sports; I admired girls at a distance, but felt uneasy about talking with them. My interest centered on science. Now, as unofficial class poet, I was invited to join the staff of the school newspaper (though I don't remember producing any more poetry worth publishing.) Classmates at least knew who I was, and the drama group even gave me a leading role as a nerdy lecturer in *Why I Am a Bachelor.*

The public doesn't value competent, dedicated teachers enough. Yet almost all of us can remember some teacher who really took an interest in passing knowledge and acceptance on to the next generation.

The Class of 1960 Nottingham High School dedicated its yearbook to Miss Smith. (She would have reached retirement about then):

"DEDICATION; We, the Class of 1960, proudly dedicate this Bulldog to you, MISS FREDERICA SMITH, our teacher, our advisor. and our friend. Soon after the portals of Nottingham were first opened you unselfishly devoted your time, effort, and ability to the students of Nottingham High School. As head of the English department, you have attained and maintained excellence in the instruction and in the study of our language. For several years you were the advisor of the Citizen. Many are the alumni who return to thank you for giving your precious time for individual explanation. You have proved to be a wonderful friend by showing personal interest in the progress and achievements of every Nottingham student. The shining improvements you have instituted in Nottingham will remain forever. We sadly think of your leaving Nottingham. We hope you keep this yearbook as a symbol of our gratitude for all you have done for us, and we join with all those you have inspired, in wishing you a happy and successful future."

Chapter 6

HAROLD SCHOCK: NOT IN MY BACKYARD, YOU SAY?

Harold and Estelle Schock, my contemporaries on the Burma mission field, were a year or two older than Lois and I. He was one of my first patients in Asia. One night Estelle knocked on our door and reported that her husband had severe abdominal pain; and asked if I would take a look at him? I went to their house across the street, talked to him, gently felt his abdomen, and decided he did not appear to have appendicitis.

But he and I had been part of a small group that had just returned from up-country by train the previous day, and I recalled his imitation of a railroad station fruit vendor. He had appeared on the station platform outside my open train window, a big grin on his face and a stalk of bananas balanced on his head, calling Ngepyawthi yadeh! ngepyawthi! (bananas! I have bananas!) and now I began to put two and two together. "Harold, how many bananas have you eaten today?"

"Lots," his wife said.

"Thirty-four," he admitted, "but they weren't very big ones."

He was that kind of guy, concentrating on ideas of the moment. I once watched him practice picking up a glass marble with a pair of chopsticks one-handed until he finally got it. (Try it yourself!)

When all foreigners, including missionaries, were expelled from Burma (now renamed Myanmar) in the 1960s, the Schocks were re-deployed to Hong Kong, and I and my family to Thailand. The former British colony of Hong Kong is comparable in size and population to greater New York City, and has as many problems with its inner-city youth.

Hong Kong changed constantly in the 1960s and 70s. Large numbers of Chinese fled there from communist mainland China in those days. When my family and I stopped in Hong Kong for a two-day visit on our way to the US in 1962, the main problem seemed to be homeless newcomers. One of the ministries of the Christian churches at that time provided food for them. The churches operated a noodle factory, famous in subsequent years for having turned out "millions of miles of noodles."

Three years after that, when the Schocks transferred out of Burma to Hong Kong, the greatest priority was providing housing and schools for recent

Chinese settlers. The government had built dozens of high-rise buildings to house them, one or two rooms per family. Many such buildings had schools on their roofs—no other place nearby to put them—and Harold supervised extra activities at three such schools: Chuck Yuen, Moon Luk, and Diamond Hill. Kindergartens, sports, supervised studies, summer day camps and field trips, Bible classes, all were part of his ministry.

These programs put him in daily contact with youth, and he gradually collected a group of young men who were drug addicts. Heroin was the main drug on the streets. He and his colleagues patiently worked with the addicts, but in the city environment it was easy for them to slide back. He needed a place to shelter them from drug dealers, and so he approached the Chinese churches.

They wanted nothing to do with a project that might endanger their own children, and firmly rejected his requests for space. At first he expanded the Chuk Yuen Christian Center into the now empty noodle factory next door, but that didn't change their environment. He appealed to Mission Headquarters in USA. They, too, told him to give up the idea. He persisted. If his work was not acceptable in city churches, he would move it out to a more rural setting.

By 1970, he raised enough local money to lease an area on a small peninsula (there are some rural parts of Hong Kong's territory) and cleared land to build a small village, Long Ke, around a former Roman Catholic Chapel. Isolated enough to prevent easy access to drugs, Long Ke originally had no road; the only access was by boat. At first, the chapel had room enough for 28 men, including a staff of five, led by a young Chinese, Johnson Ngai, in his mid-twenties. His own history included two years of primary education and five years of heroin addiction. By 1983, the Hong Kong government granted land near the chapel and approved the building of four small dormitories. By now forty young men lived at Long Ke, some in borrowed tents, plus twenty graduates living in a half-way rehab center back in the city.

By 1987 Wu Oi (roughly translated "loving friend") Christian Center had added a new dining center and kitchen, completing their site. The Center enabled drug addicts, ex-prisoners, triad [gang] members, and problem youth to return to society through Christian drug rehabilitation. Another site, four miles away, ministered to prostitutes and female addicts.

Johnson Ngai later entered a Hong Kong seminary as a special student. Four of his staff members followed him into seminaries over the next several years.

Later, Harold took teams to teach Christian drug rehabilitation in Myanmar and Thailand.

Toward the end of his work in Hong Kong, he received a Queen Elizabeth Medal for the work he had developed (Hong Kong was still a British colony in those days.) Ordinarily, the medal is intended only for British citizens, but in actual practice, each British domain is allotted a certain number of the medals, to be distributed at the discretion of the local government. Thus, the award came from the government of Hong Kong in recognition for Wu Oi's rehabilitation work.

Harold died in 1989, but the work he began continues to expand in the 21st century.

Chapter 7

CARRIE STUART PARKS, FORENSIC ARTIST
"She has a pencil, and she's not afraid to use it!

Ms. Parks reproduces a criminal's face from the description given to her by a witness or victim of the crime.

When she was studying fine arts in college, her father was the director of the School of Law Enforcement at North Idaho College, as well as head of the North Idaho Regional Crime Lab. Curiosity about some of the cases her father described led her to experiment with drawing faces from other people's description. She later took formal training from the FBI [Federal Bureau of Investigation] in 1985, and was soon being consulted by police departments seeking to identify robbers, carjackers, rapists and other assorted criminals. She has a system of detailed questioning which, together with her knowledge of facial characteristics, is often successful in getting the attention of some TV watcher or newspaper reader who can supply a name. She and her husband

Rick now teach classes in forensic art in many parts of the USA and the world at large.

I first met her through her membership in the local chapter of PEO [Philanthropic Educational Organization—also known by irreverent husbands as "Phone Each Other"] to which my wife also belongs. Carrie recently branched out into writing crime fiction with her first novel, *A Cry From the Dust*, featuring a forensic artist who reproduces a victim's likeness from a long-buried skull. (This is an allied art form, made prominent by Frank Bender's work on previously unidentified corpses in Pennsylvania and a series of murdered women in Mexico. Bender's career is recounted in Ted Botha's book, *The Girl With the Crooked Nose*.)

I interviewed Carrie at her home in December, 2014; she lives about twelve miles from my own home in Shoshone County, Idaho. She has a rustic-appearing house, on a rural dirt road. Inside, it seems larger, tastefully decorated in keeping with the couple's well-paying jobs, and shared with several rather large dogs eager to make friends.

I had just finished reading her novel, a good example of the faith-based fiction genre of which I am a fan. A Cry From the Dust is the first of a trilogy; the second will be released in the fall of 2015. We chatted about the gap between secular editors, for whom the style is not always lurid enough, and some Christian editors who forbid any overt sex scenes or foul language, but permit as many murders as the author wishes. She said one of her characters had used the mild oath "criminy". Her editor objected, finally allowed it, but specified that it could be used only once.

Carrie is a protégée of Frank Peretti, another bestselling Christian author who once resided in Idaho's Silver Valley. At present she is following the full best-seller protocol of being edited by several specialists, book-signing tours, media interviews, etc. Hence the delay before release of her second book, The Bones Will Speak, (Harper Collins/Thomas Nelson) already written but now being vetted by the editor boffins.

She has published several non-fiction works on drawing people's faces realistically.

Carrie says her career has been a series of highs in the various creative fields she has ventured into. She is an accomplished painter in watercolor and in portraits. Her law enforcement teaching accomplishments brought her the First Educator of the Year Award from Lewis Clark State College Alumni Association. The Federal Law Enforcement Academy marked her with runner-up status to their Trainer of the Year. Now that she is writing fiction, two major publishing houses had a bidding war to see who would acquire her forthcoming two novels. In all the creative fields she has entered, she finds her faith to be her inspiration.

Faith-based Christian fiction can serve as a bridge to those readers who don't take an active interest in religion, and are often turned off by those who outspokenly do. Depending on plot and writer's voice, Christian fiction can be a non-threatening introduction to a way of life to which the reader has not previously given much thought.

But Carrie Stuart Parks' profession as a competent and sympathetic forensic artist is a ministry in its own right. She enables the victim of a crime to take an active part in the identification and arrest of his/her assailant. Carrie's work can reassure an injured person that someone is actually listening, and working to achieve justice. Her influence continues to spread.

Chapter 8

ROSALIE WHITE, RADIO LICENSE K1STO

My brother Bruce and I learned Morse code—a series of dots and dashes used to send messages by telegraph or short wave radio—in our days as Boy Scouts. Bruce went on to enlist in the 10th Mountain Division (ski troops) as a radio operator in World War II, skiing with his backpack plus a 40-pound two-way radio. As the war went on, he was re-assigned to the Office of Strategic Services (OSS) west of Aachen, on the German border, to receive coded messages from agents inside German-occupied territory.

A high school student at the time, I would listen to short-wave radio Morse code late at night, but never mastered it well enough to become an amateur radio operator.

But sixty years later, completing a memoir of my fifty-year medical career and signing off on the final manuscript, I emailed the finished product to my author assistant, Rosalie White at iUniverse publishers. On a nostalgic whim, I ended the e-mail with the Morse code signal for "end of work; *di-di-dit-dah-dit-dah* [..._._]

She emailed an immediate reply, "Are you an amateur radio operator?"

I answered, "Never got licensed. You?"

She emailed back, "Extra class K1STO" [pronounced K-one-S-T-O] I researched that radio call sign, and found a news release from the American Radio Relay League when the Columbia Space Shuttle exploded in 2003:

"ARRL Field and Educational Services Manager Rosalie White, K1STO, who's been closely associated with the Space Amateur Radio Experiment (SAREX) and Amateur Radio on the International Space Station (ARISS) programs, expressed shock and sorrow over the Columbia disaster." It went on to say that three of the seven astronauts who died in the tragedy had been amateur radio operators.

Another article, apparently written for public school students, included a picture of her wearing a lineman's safety belt while up on the thirty-foot tower that supported the radio antenna above her house.

We rarely see how multidimensional the people are with whom we work. Ms. White grew up on her family's farm in southern Indiana, the youngest of three daughters, each a valedictorian in high school.

All of the family were musical, and at four years old she, together with her sisters, formed a trio, called The White Tonettes, singing three-part harmony at shows and many churches in surrounding counties. She was active in 4-H club in her youth; got a BS in Science from Indiana University and became a teacher in the Indianapolis public elementary schools, with special interest in science.

Her husband introduced her to "ham" radio, a term for the world-wide network of independent amateur radio operators. She learned Morse code, necessary at that time for an operator's license. When her husband got a job at the American Radio Relay League headquarters in Connecticut, she found that no teachers' jobs were open in the public schools there. So she too, applied for a job at ARRL and within a few months qualified as a novice, upgrading through the years to General Class, finally reaching the highest level of the Extra Class with the call sign K1STO.

She is one of thousands across the world, who operated two-way long-distance radios, long before the advent of e-mail and the Internet. One of her early duties included verifying the records of members of the DX Century Club, operators who had contacted at least one hundred distant (DX) overseas amateur radio operators. Soon promoted to assistant to the emergency communications manager, she trained amateur operators to set up emergency sites in times of national disasters when conventional communication fails.

Six months later she was promoted again, to lead the ARRL affiliated Club Program, some 2,000 amateur radio clubs across the US. She helped develop new clubs, maintained a film library on technical topics, connected inquirers to radio-license instructors, and student clubs to school teachers with amateur radio experience. By this time she was also writing a column for emergency radio operators in the ARRL's monthly magazine, *QST*.

In 1975, ARRL combined Rosalie's several duties into a single new department for clubs, instructors, and public relations. She produced study manuals, workbooks and teachers guides. She was named assistant manager, and a year later became manager when her predecessor stepped down. Her increasing duties put a strain on her marriage which contributed to a divorce.

Three years later, she left ARRL, and she and her new husband started an electronics company, manufacturing pre-amplifiers to enhance radio reception. The company proved successful, supplying a product with increasing demand from the radio industry. But working with her husband 24/7 again put increasing strain on her marriage. She stepped away from the company after about five years, and in 1985, on ARRL's invitation, rejoined her previous department.

The job now included education of ham radio instructors, and schoolteachers bringing radio into the classroom. The department oversaw state-level

ARRL managers, emergency communications networks, and memorandums of understanding with FEMA, Red Cross, Scouts, and other groups. She also guided special ARRL members nationwide who monitored for illegal radio transmissions, for the Federal Communications Commission.

It was about this time that Rosalie took up flying as a recreation. The company she had helped start was located next to a small airport, and she soon met the licensing requirements for small planes, enjoying the camaraderie of local pilots, especially with the ten or twelve female pilots in the group. She still regards flying as the peak of her career, and spent fifteen satisfying years flying.

She served as ARRL's representative to the amateur radio manufacturing industry during this period. In addition, because of her background in education and working with technicians, Rosalie's boss asked her to be ARRL's rep for SAREX (Shuttle Amateur Radio EXperiment) to connect school children in the classroom directly with astronauts in orbit, with the hope of interesting more students in science, technology and math subjects. This work helped her earn the Dayton Hamvention Amateur of the Year in 1995, the highest award in amateur radio.

As the International Space Station was being built, she at ARRL and team mates at NASA created Amateur Radio on the International Space Station (ARISS). This moved USA's SAREX program to international status and, as one of the two American delegates to ARISS, she was voted ARISS International Secretary-Treasurer, a voluntary post she still holds.

After her father died, the needs of her aging mother (in assisted living) brought her back to Bloomington, Indiana, where she manages reduced ARRL work from home. Increasing medical expenses made it advisable to get a full-time local job, which she did at iUniverse, a publishing company headquartered in Bloomington. It was then that I first met her, when she was assigned as author assistant for my book-length memoir *Bridge Ahead*, in 2008.

She has since moved to the parent company of iUniverse, Author Solutions, where she is now a custom illustrations coordinator.

In interviewing her, I was surprised to hear her say that she looks at herself as a generalist, not a specialist.

KD: To me, International Secretary-Treasurer of Amateur Radio on the International Space Station (ARISS), maintaining contact between today's Astronauts and tomorrow's generation of student scientists and engineers is a very specialized mission indeed?

RW: I consider my primary achievement in life to be earning my pilot's license and owning a plane, doing regular small maintenance tasks under the tutelage of FAA-licensed mechanics. It is my biggest regret that I can no longer pilot a plane because of the expense involved.

KD: With all three of you sisters each a valedictorian, your family is apparently blessed with a superior gene pool. What other life interests have you had?

RW: We still sing together, mostly at family gatherings. And I am a space nut, fascinated by astronomy, telescopes, meteor showers and other events in the sky, and all things NASA.

KD: I hear nostalgia when you speak about flying, and about singing with your sisters. You haven't said much about your "day jobs". It sounds like you have succeeded at both ARRL and at AuthorSolutions; have you any special regrets or joys about your career? Or life in general?

RW: My favorite ARRL project was SAREX-leading-to-ARISS, plus traveling all over US for forums and workshops at conventions. At Author Solutions I have worked with many talented and dedicated team mates and interesting authors. Doing new things and learning new things are good. My mother influenced me about the importance of education.

KD: Looking back, who do you regard as your mentors?

RW: My dad was my number-one hero; he had a curiosity that wouldn't stop, and he instilled that in his three daughters. And my first boss at ARRL, Ellen White (no relation to me) who guided me well. She earned her amateur radio license and her commercial radio license, becoming a commercial broadcast station engineer in the 1940s—unheard of for a woman then!

KD: Do you still keep personal contact with many amateur radio operators? Are there as many operators in the 21st century, after the coming of Facebook, Twitter, LinkedIn, and all?

RW: Amateur radio growth in the US continues to increase. The Federal Communication Commission's Universal Licensing System database reached an all-time high at the end of 2014 of 726,275 amateur operators, and now [2015] exceeds 727,000. In recent years I've gone to see amateur radio friends all over the US. I have logged contacts in 124 countries. My most memorable was a brief contact with a ham in Franz Josef Land [in the Arctic Ocean at 81 degrees north latitude, far north of Russia.]

KD: Has the role of amateur radio changed in modern disasters like the Nepal quake or the plight of refugees?

RW: In years past, amateur radio was usually on the scene for several weeks at major disasters. These days, amateur radio usually stays on-scene for 24 hours until portable commercial communications are set up. When cell phone batteries die, there is nowhere to recharge them in wilderness areas. But once a year, on Field Day, thousands of hams set up portable stations with generators or solar power, and improvised antennas, to see if they can still handle emergency communications.

KD: Any advice to young student scientists or mathematicians nowadays?

RW: The same advice given by so many astronauts—whatever you enjoy in school, focus on it and get very good at it. And along the way learn a little about a lot of things.

Chapter 9

GORDON SEAGRAVE: THE BURMA SURGEON

Gordon Seagrave, MD, a graduate of Johns Hopkins Medical School, was a tough surgeon of the old breed. At the beginning of World War II, he walked 200 miles out of Burma to India as General Stilwell's chief medical officer, ahead of the advancing Japanese army. After the war, he rebuilt his hospital in northern Burma (now Myanmar) with truckloads of grapefruit-size stone, hand-picked from the riverbed. He had an excellent, nation-wide reputation, both for his surgery and the school of nursing he established. In my high school days, Seagrave was one of my heroes, the ideal surgeon.

Not long after I first arrived in Burma in 1957, the mission sent me on a week's visit to see Dr. Seagrave and to learn how a small-town hospital is run. The plan was for me to fly to Lashio and meet an up-country missionary there who would drive me the remaining 120 miles to Namkham. Instead, I got a chance to see how well I could manage alone on only one month of language study, after discovering that the missionary wasn't in town.

At Lashio, the Union of Burma Airways agent drove me from the airport into town and put me on a bus to Kutkai, about halfway to Namkham. Burmese buses of that era were converted weapons carriers left over from World War II, with a single plank on which to sit on each side of the back. Crates, sacks of rice, oil drums and other freight occupied the aisle in between. Looking forward from where I sat with my feet wedged between two crates, I could see a passenger in the front seat who, at each sharp curve on the one-lane mountain road, touched two bare wires together to sound the horn.

The man sitting next to me looked car-sick and ready to throw up. I offered him a Dramamine pill, and we were able to communicate a few syllables now and then. After a three-hour trip to cover forty-two miles, we reached Kutkai and the driver let me off at the mission gate. The missionary couple who lived there were on leave in America, but fortunately the housekeeper spoke English. A VW minibus took me the rest of the way to Namkham next day, arriving in mid-afternoon at the house of Dr. Albert Ail Lun, Dr. Seagrave's associate, who took me to meet him.

Seagrave looked old and ill as he sat at his desk. He didn't even look up, but made some grumpy remark about damn tourists. I mentioned that he had stayed at our house in Syracuse some years before, and he then turned to me with a crooked grin on his tired face and growled, "Well why didn't you say so?" We got along well after that.

During the next four days, I looked at everything from kitchen to operating rooms, learning their record-keeping system, pharmacy management, nursing classes, and sanitation. The hospital itself consisted of four stone buildings, two stories each, housing a total of 250 patients, surrounded by nurses' dormitories, repair shops, houses, and a church. I listened to Seagrave teach as he slumped in a chair, his chin jutting out, questioning each student, trying to get her to think rather than just memorize. Class over, he would trudge up to the operating room, or to make patient rounds.

Many doctors visited Namkham Hospital each year, and Dr. Seagrave made each one scrub in on some surgical procedure, no exceptions or excuses, not even for internists or psychiatrists. My assignment was a difficult delivery. He applied obstetric forceps and then stood back to puff on the cigarette always held lit and ready by a nurse. "Deliver the baby, Doctor." he said.

I gave an experimental pull; the baby's head was jammed tightly within the woman's small pelvis. "I don't think this a case for forceps, Dr. Seagrave," I said apologetically.

"Pull, dammit!" he said.

With misgivings and considerable physical effort, I

followed his order and extracted the baby, alive but in obvious shock. I spent maybe fifteen minutes trying to resuscitate it, as the attentive nurse stood by with an "I expected this" look on her face. Dr. Seagrave had left the room. Finally, having failed to restore any sign of life, I pronounced the baby dead.

Dr. Ai Lun was furious when he heard. "I told Dr. Seagrave, that patient had lost three children in childbirth and that she needed a C-section, and he said there wasn't time!"

I had mixed feelings about the old doctor. My being used as a tool in some spat with one of his assistant doctors that day was an inexcusable tragedy for the baby's mother, but it did not change my recognition of his past accomplishments.

You have to understand what surgeons were like in mid-twentieth-century America, self-sufficient pioneers of their craft, masters of a field that other men barely comprehended, admired for their successes, with few to question their failures. Even in America, surgeons were the elite. Nurses stood up when a surgeon entered a room. Dr. Seagrave had trained at the premiere medical school of his day. He maintained high standards of surgery in a foreign land at a time when many doctors there were quacks, or rejects from more advanced nations. When I opened the hospital in Kengtung the following year, Dr. Seagrave sent me two excellent nurse-midwives from Namkham, Nang Shwe Yin (a Shan) and Maran Lu Seng (a Kachin.)

He saved lives from all over Burma, but he was unable to revive his own son when the boy was discovered after he drowned in a nearby lake. His wife had finally refused to accompany him back to Burma after a stateside furlough, but still he went back. That was the mindset of many missionaries of that era—you were in this for your whole life—"He who is not willing to give up lands and family is not fit for the Kingdom of God."

He must have smoked three packs a day, and a bad heart required him to ride in a car between hospital buildings, yet he scorned all advice that he needed to rest. He still supervised the weekly baseball game that he required all student nurses to take part in. And in a nation where typical medical treatment was a shot of calcium gluconate, people came 600 miles from Rangoon to have their surgery in Namkham. When the Burma government once placed him under house arrest for alleged treason (a charge later dismissed by the Burmese Supreme Court), he performed successful surgery in his home on the kitchen table.

A couple of years after my visit, the wife of another doctor wrote a book, *The Devil in God's Old Man*. I thought it a sad but vivid description of the old doctor. But I prefer to remember what his life achieved by recalling a verse from a hymn sung that Sunday morning in Namkham, Felix Adler's *Hail the Glorious Golden City*:

And the work that we have builded,
Oft with bleeding hands and tears,
Oft in error, oft in anguish,
Will not perish with our years:
It will live and shine transfigured,
In the final reign of Right;
It will pass into the splendors
Of the city of the light.

Some say that hymn does not belong in a Christian hymnbook. But God is sometimes inscrutable when He chooses who writes the hymns or who builds the hospitals.

All my five years as a solo doctor in isolated Kengtung, I still aspired to be as skilled as he. But his personality was a factor in my not wanting to grow old on the foreign mission field.

Chapter   10

LUCY BALIAN RORKE-ADAMS: HOW DO THE CHILDREN DIE?

Lucy Balian and I were the same age, kids together in First Baptist Church's Sunday school in St. Paul, Minnesota. She was youngest of five sisters; I was youngest of three siblings. When our families occasionally got together, we two were the smallest, occupied with our own interests, not older folks' conversation. We last saw each other at the age of ten, when my family moved to Syracuse, New York. As it happened, Lucy and I both became doctors, but different kinds.

Lucy's family came from Turkey, where her father, Aram Balian, worked on the section of the Berlin to Baghdad railroad that went through Turkey. When that section of railroad was completed in 1913, his German boss advised him that persecution of the Armenian minority by the Turks was growing more severe, and he offered to take Aram to Germany with him. Aram had no interest in Germany, but told his two brothers and brother-in-law what was to take place. They left for America, eventually settling in Minneapolis, where Aram worked as a skilled cabinet maker for a Ford Motor Company subsidiary. He began seeking a wife. A friend knew a friend in Constantinople (now Istanbul) who knew of a young Armenian lady who might be interested in emigrating to America. Aram sent her a letter, with his picture.

Lucy's mother miraculously survived the genocide of the Armenians by the Turks. Her two sisters and brother also survived, although her brother had been bought as a slave by a Turk. She was saved by a chance encounter with a group of Turkish women seeking a seamstress to make a trousseau for an upcoming wedding. She had learned the art of French dressmaking, and it saved her life. She was protected by a number of Turkish families after that, and at the end of the the first world war, she moved to Constantinople in relative safety.

When Aram Balian sent that letter, she answered with her own picture. His second letter contained a proposal of marriage. In March of 1921 they met at Ellis Island, the New York entry point for immigrants, were married a week later, and made their home in Minneapolis. They had five daughters: Eva, the oldest, Harriet, Maline, Elizabeth, and Lucy, who was born in 1929. That was the year the Great

Depression began, and Aram lost his job.

Lucy pursued music at first. In the 1940s, in her teens, she hoped to be an opera singer. A friend recommended her to Metropolitan Opera diva Gladys Swarthout, who was looking for a protégée. Lucy's friend arranged an audition with Miss Swarthout in Chicago.

"The plan was to take a train to Chicago, attend the operas and have the audition," Lucy told me. "You can imagine my excitement. My mother had sewed me a most gorgeous white taffeta evening gown—the most beautiful dress I had ever encountered. Well, the day before we were to depart, my friend got a call from Miss Swarthout who said she was ill (heart failure from childhood rheumatic heart disease) and she had canceled her trip to Chicago. I was devastated! After the initial shock and tears receded, I decided that being an opera singer was not part of God's plan for my life. It was about that time that I came upon a copy of Lloyd Douglas' book, The Magnificent Obsession.

This is the story of a feckless young playboy who accidentally causes the death of a famous neurosurgeon. This marks a turning point in his life as he decides to become a neurosurgeon himself, and carry on in the same profession of the one whose life was lost. I was so deeply impressed that I decided to pursue a career in medicine."

Lucy studied at the University of Minnesota medical school, and chose an internship at the 1,800-

bed Philadelphia General Hospital "Actually I was captivated by neurosurgery and might have become one save for the fact that during my internship I discovered that I did not function too well without much sleep. And since the life of a surgeon is characterized by sleep deprivation I reconsidered that goal. Anyway, my career in neuropathology has been fantastic, so all has worked out well."

She took her three-year residency in pathology at PGH, moving on to a fellowship in neuropathology from 1961-1962, and became chairman of the department in 1969, gradually focusing on very highly specialized work as a pediatric neuro-pathologist (dealing with development of the infant brain, and injuries and tumors of the brain in children.) The choice of pediatric sub-specialty was not entirely hers. She remembers that on the first day of residency training, the chief pathologist surveyed the incoming group of residents and told her, "You're the only girl here, and since pediatrics is the province of ladies, you have to do all the children's autopsies." She accepted the challenge, and for the next twenty years often performed 500 or more autopsies per year plus examining surgical specimens of tumors, nerves, and muscles.

In 1965, Lucy also joined the staff of Children's Hospital of Philadelphia (CHOP). And when Philadelphia's mayor closed Philadelphia General Hospital in 1977, she moved to CHOP, becoming president of its medical staff nine years later. Her focus on child abuse cases and brain tumors in children has required her to travel often to consult on unexplained deaths of infants and children in many hospitals in America and Europe. Asked how many autopsies she has done in the past fifty-two years, she estimates 25,000 brains. If the famous murder case of JonBenet Ramsey in 1996 had ever come to trial, Lucy would have been one of the expert witnesses involved.

Her marriage to her first husband lasted 42 years until his death. She married again at age 75, but her husband survived for only two years. Seven years later she married a third time to C. Harry Knowles, a physicist and inventor. One of his most widely-used inventions is the hand-held bar-code reader.

She still worked up to twelve hours per day at age 85, arriving at her office at 4:30 a.m. after a seventeen mile drive from her home. She generally quit at 2:00 p.m. except every third week, when she was on call for seven straight days. She retired on July 2, 2015, after serving as neuropathologist for the Children's Hospital of Philadelphia for 50 years. Over her long career Lucy's work involved many areas of research, including childhood brain tumors, developmental defects, vaccines, multiple sclerosis, child abuse and, of course, training the next generation of doctors.

She had in her keeping a set of microscope slides of Albert Einstein's brain, which she gifted to the Mutter Museum of the College of Physicians of Philadelphia in 2012.

She is most proud of the legacy of the Lucy Balian Rorke-Adams Chair of Pediatric Neuropathology established by The Children's Hospital on the occasion of her 80th birthday.

Chapter 11

LAURAN BETHELL: FIGHTING HUMAN TRAFFICKING

Two young ladies, Lauran Bethell and Judy Butler, visited our hospital and our home in Thailand in July, 1979. American school teachers in Hong Kong at the time, they had a few days of vacation and wanted to see mission work. My wife and I had a pleasant day or two with them, after which they continued their tour of several Thai mission stations.

Unknown to us at the time, Lauran was suffering bouts of severe depression, soon made worse when she developed dengue fever, causing her to cut her trip short and return to Hong Kong. The illness and her own lack of self-esteem had brought her to emotional desolation. She considered suicide.

One evening, she called out to God in a desperate prayer—doubting that God would hear her or was even there. She begged that the sadness, inadequacy and worthlessness she felt be taken away. She told

God that if her depression disappeared, she would tell everyone that it was God's work, and do whatever she could to help others who suffered in this way.

She really didn't think that anything would happen, and went to sleep that night thinking about throwing herself off her 15th story balcony.

Next morning, slowly waking up, with her eyes still closed, she felt as if the room was filled with the presence she can only describe as "angels singing the most heavenly music, repeating over and over, "You're okay, You're okay, You're okay." Over and over and over. And in those moments she knew that God had healed her. The words told her that she didn't have to feel that she was worse—or better— than anyone around her. She was okay, created in God's image. She knew that God had a purpose for her, and that she only had to live into that purpose.

She continued teaching at the Hong Kong International School for the next 3 years, growing in her new confidence. The point came when she knew she should leave teaching and embark on a new challenge—though she didn't know what that would be. One evening, she was with missionary friends who invited her to "come and join us". She felt honored that they thought she could be a missionary —but she just knew she could never do that. She didn't think she was smart enough, or wise enough— and she certainly couldn't speak other languages, or even learn them! Throughout the following weekend, those words just kept going around and around in her mind "come and join us, come and join us". But, she thought, I don't have the skills or the smarts.

That Sunday morning, during the last words of a hymn, "love so amazing, so Divine, demands my life, my soul, my all," she realized that wherever she felt inadequate to the task, God would provide the gifts and resources needed.

Following three years of seminary, in 1985 she was appointed as a member of a new pioneering team teaching English in cooperation with the Church in China. She had fallen in love with "all things Chinese" during her years in Hong Kong, and knew that this new adventure was truly God's Call, using her gifts and skills and passion.

But shortly after arriving in China, she developed an excruciatingly painful back problem and had to return to the USA for surgery. During her recovery, she learned that she could not go back to China because someone else had taken her position during her absence. She felt devastated, but wanted to get on with her life in Asia. She got reassigned to work in Thailand, where she was supposed to teach in a school started by an historic Chinese church in Bangkok. She had loved visiting Thailand during that trip in 1979, and though it wasn't her first choice, she decided she'd try to make it work.

First, she had to study the Thai language for a year in Bangkok. She really wanted to be studying Chinese in China—and language school was a difficult experience for her. In her heart, she couldn't understand why she was in Thailand when the Call to China had been so powerful and exciting.

Every day on her way to language school, she had to walk down Patpong Road—one of the most famous red-light districts in Bangkok. She was living with so much sadness about her dashed hopes and visions for ministry in China—and here she was, doing badly in Thai language school, walking through this horrible street every day. She began to look into the faces of the women standing in front of the bars, and questioned in her mind why they were there, working in prostitution. In the midst of her angst in language school, she decided to embark on a research project to answer that question. She contacted as many Thai women's organizations as she could to find out what they were doing about prostitution issues. She also volunteered with a secular organization to teach English to prostitutes on Patpong Road. She wanted an opportunity to hear their stories.

What she learned in her research shocked her. The women told her that they were working in prostitution to support their parents, or siblings; or sometimes their own children. "We are sacrificing ourselves for the sake of our family," they would tell her—often using that word "sacrifice". From her own Western "individualistic" culture, she would never have considered sacrificing herself in such a way. Rather, her parents were expected to support her! But she learned that in these "community-based" cultures from which the Thai women came, what they were doing by prostituting themselves to send money to build homes, or send siblings to school, was considered "noble". Their value and worth came from what they could do to support their family.

Her realizations about the root causes and motivations for working in prostitution in Thailand begged the question "what are the alternatives?" There were none offered in 1986 to young women with little or no education and a desperate need to support their families.

She became increasingly angry about the situation, and one day wrote a very bitter prayer to God in her journal: "You know that I'm miserable here—I really want to be in China. I'm questioning Your Will for my life. The one thing that I want to do here is to somehow help the women and girls to have alternatives to working in prostitution. But I'm supposed to teach English in a nice boarding school. Okay, God, I will fulfill my 3-year commitment to do that—but just know that during these next three years, I will be miserable—and after three years You'd better have something better for me—and it needs to be something that helps the women to have alternatives to prostitution. So there." She slammed her journal shut—and actually felt better about life in Thailand!

She didn't have to wait three years. About six weeks later, colleagues of Lois and me, Paul and Elaine Lewis, called Lauran. Paul and Elaine had been serving the hill tribe communities of Akha and Lahu people in Myanmar and Northern Thailand for more than forty years. In this phone conversation, they told her how concerned they were with the number of young hill tribe girls going to the cities for "good jobs to support their families", and instead being tricked and sold into prostitution. Once involved, the young girl is kept against her will. She is unprotected against AIDS and other venereal diseases, may be physically beaten to make her obey, and often has only a hopeless and brief life to look forward to. Paul and Elaine knew that they needed to do something to address the root causes: the need to support families, and the lack of education and vocational skills. Elaine had brought together a small committee of hill tribe women who decided to start a project called "The New Life Center", offering at-risk tribal girls the opportunity for an education and vocational training. Lauran listened intently as Paul and Elaine described their vision for the Center over the phone. And then they asked Lauran, "We'd like to know if you have any interest in coming to be the director of this project?" Paul and Elaine had no idea, 400 miles north of Bangkok, that Lauran had been carrying out her research project, or had prayed her angry prayer to God. All they knew is that as they were praying about possibilities for the Center, Lauran's name kept coming to their minds, and they had to call to see if she might be willing to come north?

Lois and I were back in the USA at that time, but

in 1989 on a visit to the city of Chiang Mai in Thailand, we met Lauran again. By this time, she was running three shelter houses for girls and women rescued from the forced sex trade, and for women who had come to Chiang Mai to hunt for a job. These shelters gave women a safe place to stay, night-school classes and job training. They had access to medical treatment if needed, as well as the company of others in the same situation, and exposure to Christian life. The three houses together had room for about sixty at any one time.

The project continued to expand, and when the Center celebrated its10th anniversary in 1997, there was room for more than 150 residents. In addition, the New Life Center offered scholarship aid and oversight for at-risk girls to be able to attend schools in their own villages. They also organized teams of residents to go into villages, performing dramas and offering information to prevent vulnerable villagers from being trafficked. One such drama *The Prodigal Daughter*, attracted an outdoor audience of more than 500 in our hospital's town of Mae Sariang.

When Lauran began her research in 1986, she found no other organization in Thailand offering direct intervention and service to girls and women working in prostitution. Since then, increasing numbers of individuals have felt called to begin such projects in many dark corners of the world. Often, they came to seek advice and to learn from Lauran's experience.

In recent years, American Baptist International Ministries has established "global consultants", traveling specialists teaching clean water supply, or education, or farming, etc., and Lauran now works all over the world as consultant in human trafficking, a polite term for combating sex slavery. Her home base is currently outside of Amsterdam in the Netherlands. She serves by encouraging and facilitating Christ-based ministries that address the exploitation of women and children. She writes:

I often walk through red-light districts in cities that I visit. I'm never comfortable being there, but I know that these are the places where God has called me to be present, despite being uneasy. While walking amidst the customers, the pimps, the women and men selling sexual services, I continually remind myself that all of them have been created in God's image. After all these years of working with these issues, I still have to stare through the evil that has distorted God's gift of sexuality, and chant these words over and over to myself: "Every one of them is precious in God's sight. God longs for them to know the love that created them."

Impossible, you might think, that God's love could break into that stronghold of evil in red-light districts, strip clubs, or pornographic movies. Impossible.

When we opened the New Life Center in Chiang Mai, Thailand, in 1987, I knew it was important for those first 18 girls to know Christ, to receive an education and to be prevented from having to support their families by being exploited. I had no idea that God had much grander plans to reach the strongholds of evil and shine the Light into the darkness. What God brought into being those twenty-plus years ago brought hope to hundreds of girls and young women. And from that tiny beginning, God has multiplied the ministry beyond the bounds of what any of us could have imagined.

And in a more recent article:

I was feeling insecure as I headed towards a speaking engagement in Finland. I hadn't known how to prepare, because not even the organizers knew what to expect from the event. They only knew that God was prompting them to raise awareness about human trafficking in their community. We had no idea what God would do with our efforts.

We were amazed when twice as many people as expected showed up for the event from all over the country!

Apparently, God's Spirit had been moving in Finland, calling many folks to begin new projects addressing human trafficking issues. They had come to this gathering looking for information and a network. It was clear that this was God's moment—not ours! Combating human trafficking has been the goal and passion of my life ever since God called me to work in Thailand's New Life Center in 1986.

But it hasn't been my greatest challenge. Sitting down to prepare for public speaking—and silencing the voices in my mind that call me "incapable" and that say, no matter what I do, it will never be enough —that is my greatest challenge.

The experience in Finland reminded me, once again, that I don't have to be afraid of "not being enough." As I follow God's call in this ministry, I realize that God is moving in wider and deeper ways than I can imagine.

Lauran served as Director of The New Life Center in Chiang Mai, Thailand, for fourteen years. In 2001 she began her international consultant ministry, facilitating the development and increased capacity of grass-roots projects which are addressing human trafficking and prostitution. While based in The Netherlands, she travels extensively throughout Europe, Asia and the Americas, teaching, training and consulting.

In 2004, Lauran directed the first International Christian Consultation on Ministry with Women in Prostitution, bringing together the leaders of faith-based organizations from 25 countries which are involved in this work. Also in 2004, she initiated Project Hope in the Czech Republic working with Bulgarian Roma (gypsy) women involved in prostitution, many of whom are trafficked.

One of her major endeavors was the formation of a large network of grass-roots organizations called the "International Christian Alliance on Prostitution" (ICAP). This group regularly sponsors regional and international conferences, bringing together women and men who are walking into red-light districts with God's love and care, offering whatever it takes to bring healing and hope. The conferences allow these practitioners to share their burdens and joys, their creative ideas and concerns, and find spiritual and emotional refreshment to continue their ministries.

Lauran serves on the Anti-Trafficking Committee of the European Baptist Federation. She has collaborated with governmental agencies and non-government organizations, and a broad spectrum of faith-based groups. She has testified before the U.S. House and Senate committees as they drafted and revised the U.S. anti-trafficking legislation.

Human trafficking is the second-largest illegal business in the world, only surpassed by drug trafficking. Many people think that it's just too overwhelming an issue to even begin to tackle. Lauran has often felt the same way. Much of the time, she says, she "has no idea what to do". So I asked her, "How do you keep going and stay positive after nearly three decades working with such a dark subject?"

She doesn't hesitate with her answer: "I have had the privilege of watching God at work over all these years, from the first moments when I realized that the women needed alternatives to prostitution, and there were none until now, when every magazine and newspaper prints articles about what people are doing and how lives are being saved. I've seen how

God multiplied my small efforts, and those of many others, to create a world-wide movement. I've realized that ultimately, it's not my battle to fight or win—it's God's. God has called me to be faithful and has opened doors for me to walk through. I live with a grateful heart for all the amazing people I've met along the way, who have taken courageous risks and who have inspired me. It's been an amazing journey."

Chapter 12

EDWIN T. DAHLBERG, MINISTER

My father, Edwin T. Dahlberg, was a prominent figure in the mid-twentieth century. He was a leader of the Northern Baptists (now American Baptist Churches), served three years as president of the National Council of [Protestant] Churches in the USA, and was a member of the Central Committee of the World Council of Churches.

He interacted with leaders of the US Government, the Pentagon, labor unions and industry, on many issues in the 1940s to 1970s, but that's not what he's about here. I have already written a book-length biography of him and the details of all that are in it. Those who have read that biography thoughtfully can skip on to the next person in this book. For those who have not, I summarize here what Dad absorbed from his seminary professor and mentor, Walter Rauschenbusch.

In his own early career Rauschenbusch had a

ministry in one of New York City's most infamous slum neighborhoods, known as Hell's Kitchen. He became deeply involved in the lives of those caught in that whirlpool of violence, crime, failed lives, and despair. Rauschenbusch became convinced that an effective minister of the Gospel must not only minister to the soul of the individual who had lost touch with God but must also address the environment that had led the individual away from God in the first place. Most churchgoers would have agreed with this up to a point—liquor, drugs, illicit sex, and other such temptations were often-cited causes of "going astray."

But Rauschenbusch went further. High profits at the expense of low wages, slumlords who failed to maintain New York tenements, wars that drained the assets of whole nations, the industry that produced the liquor—all these and more were proper topics to be addressed by the Christian ministry.

"Evangelism and social action go together, or you don't have the Gospel!" was Rauschenbusch's constant theme, and this scraped the nerves of some who did not like to be thus disturbed. In addition, just as some preachers stuck to "saving souls," some others believed that the Kingdom of God could be ushered in by simply correcting social evils and working for a social utopia. Rauschencusch's belief that both approaches must be essential parts of any effective ministry was lost in a rising storm of arguments and mutual scorn between "fundamentalist Christians" and "liberal Christians" over the meaning

— and desirability—of the "social Gospel."

A couple of incidents stick in my memory, that place Dad among this group of people who have in various ways influenced those around them. Not that any of these people are any better than thousands of others in the human race, but they are some whom I have known personally and can describe.

In 1960, during Dad's three-year term as president of the National Council of Churches, a major story hit America's news headlines: AIR FORCE MANUAL TIES COMMIES TO CHURCHES.

Air Training Command in Texas had published 6,100 copies of a training manual for non-commissioned officers in the Air Force Reserve. 3,290 copies were distributed around the United States before Air Force Secretary Dudley Sharp ordered the manual withdrawn. Most of the manual dealt with routine security maintenance, but one chapter informed the trainees: "Communists and Communist fellow-travelers have successfully infiltrated our churches . . . It is known that even the pastors of certain of our churches are card-carrying Communists!"

Dad was chairing a meeting of the NCC Council in Oklahoma City at the time, and had to turn the chair over to the vice-chairman several times that day and exit the meeting room to answer questions from eight news reporters, and face three TV cameras.

The irate public relations department of the NCC immediately got in touch with the Defense Department and the Air Force to refute the headlines. But the manual had more to say: "Another rather foolish remark often heard is that Americans have a right to know what's going on . . . If a football team should start telling the other side the plays it planned to use, their opponents would sweep them off the field."

This angered the nation's press and universities, who saw a difference between protecting military strategy and inserting unproven political statements in a military training manual.

A debate in Congress, on April 19th, 1960 did a lot to swing public opinion to support the NCC. Both Democrats and Republicans, regardless of their personal opinions on the matter, realized that a lot of their constituents belonged to the Protestant churches that were being maligned. Debate about the manual went on in Congress for three days, some criticizing the NCC for supporting diplomatic recognition of Red China; others criticizing the Air Force for not even consulting its own department of chaplains before publishing the manual.

Oklahoma radio/TV evangelist Billy James Hargis claimed responsibility for the manual's allegations, and he posted placards around Oklahoma City that challenged Dad to a public debate: "We dare. Does he dare?" Dad declined, since the Air Force had already apologized and withdrawn the manual, and the NCC didn't want to give further publicity to the opposing groups at a time when public opinion overwhelmingly supported the NCC.

Hargis brought an entourage to St. Louis, where Dad pastored Delmar Street Baptist Church. Pleased as Dad had been with the outcome of the Air Force Manual investigation, he felt there was still one more aspect to address: reconciliation was more important than victory. "The main object in conflict," Dad often said, "is not to win the victory and eliminate the enemy, but to win the enemy and eliminate the enmity." Against all advice, he made a phone call.

Hargis's secretary picked up the phone in his hotel suite, and Dad could hear him telling his employer, "Some phony is on the line who says he's Dahlberg of the National Council of Churches!" The Oklahoma evangelist took the phone, skepticism changing to amazement, and then to wary acceptance of Dad's invitation to lunch at the University Club.

"Hargis turned out to be a pretty good egg," Dad wrote in a family letter. "I don't think I converted him to the National Council, but I believe we had a very worthwhile session. We sat and talked for four hours together, and at the end of it I said, 'Let's just have a time of prayer together.' I prayed, and at the end of it Hargis said, 'I promise you now, I will never again say a harsh word about you!' And he never did."

On August 21, 1997, I did a phone interview with Dr. Hargis about the Air Force Manual and events following. He remembered it well, saying, "Your dad was one of the best friendships I ever had . . . not an out-and-out liberal . . . [He and I] would discuss, not argue." Their long discussion that afternoon in Hargis's hotel room ended when a fire happened to break out elsewhere in the hotel. Hargis's wife and children had gone off to the zoo, except for his small son who was napping in a nearby room. Hargis and Dad led the boy down the smoke-filled hall. Neither of them speculated on what newspaper reporters (gathered with the firemen below) might have said had they known the identity of the three descending the fire escape.

The other memory I vividly recall is an afternoon in St. Louis when I had hitch-hiked from medical school in Syracuse to spend Christmas week with Mother and Dad. I was driving his car through what passes for a winter storm there in Missouri (slippery streets from an inch or two of snow), when we stopped at a railroad crossing to let a long freight train slowly roll by.

As we waited, I turned to say something to Dad and found he had disappeared, leaving the passenger-side door open. Then I saw him by the flashing red crossing lights, one hand on the shoulder of a swaying drunk. Dad stood there talking to him until the last train car had passed by, thus allowing the drunk to safely cross the tracks.

As Dad got back in the car I asked him, "What did you talk to him about?" hoping to get some tip that would prove useful back in med school.

"There wasn't much to say that the man would remember," Dad answered. "The idea now is to keep him alive, hoping he'll hear something useful when he's sober."

Dad also led me to Christ, counseled me in childhood, youth and adulthood at times when I was uncertain of the road ahead. He even asked me to be best man at his wedding, nine years after the death of my mother, Emilie, at age 75. He and Viola had nine more years of happiness until his death at age 93.

Chapter 13

PAUL LEWIS: TRANSLATOR

Paul and Elaine Lewis were my mentors during my first few years in Asia. They arrived in Burma (now Myanmar) in 1947, just two years after the end of World War II, and only a few weeks before that country gained independence from British rule. They worked among the Lahu tribe in Burma's easternmost mountains. Under local leadership, about 10,000 Christian Lahu lived in the region.

Ten years later, Lois and I and our two small daughters arrived in Burma, to restore the mission hospital in Kengtung, a town about seventeen miles from the Lewis's home in Pangwai. Kengtung had a population of about 20,000, and was the capital of Eastern Shan State. The hospital buildings were in bad condition after being used by the Japanese as a command post, and then strafed by American warplanes.

On December 10, 1957, the old DC-3 plane of the

Union of Burma Airways landed at Kengtung's airstrip. Armed Burmese soldiers stood guard at the perimeter against possible attack by insurgent forces. Paul and Elaine met us there to greet us and help us get settled in town.

Unlike Lois and me, Paul and Elaine were expert linguists, fluent in Burmese and Lahu, and had a speaking knowledge of Shan. They were then studying Akha, the language of another hill group. In the pecking order of Burma, the Burmans looked down on the Shan, who looked down on the Lahu, who looked down on the Akha. Each ethnic group had its own language and culture, but the fairly intricate language of the Akha people had never been written. Paul was able to put this tonal language into written form, using a phonemic script. The Lahu had a middle school at Pangwai, taught in their own language as well as in Burmese. The school principal was an educated Lahu man named Sala Ai Pun.

The Lahu people had only a rough translation of the New Testament before World War II. During the war the printing plates got so mixed up they could not be used. The Lahu leaders asked Paul to head up a team to do a totally new translation. He worked four years with two Lahu Seminary graduates and Sala Ai Pun to make the translation. The task was complicated by the fact that Lahu syllables can be spoken in seven different tones. If the wrong tone is used the meaning can be very different. This translation is now used by Lahu Christians in China, Burma, Thailand and Laos.

Meanwhile Paul, who had soaked up as much of the Akha language as possible, started work on the translation of the New Testament into the Akha language. A different set of helpers had to be chosen by the Akha leaders. Paul has confessed to me that translation work is very challenging, since you are seeking to find the equivalent meaning in Akha of the expression from the original Greek.

The Lahu Bible (including the Old Testament) is now being printed by the Amity Foundation in Nanjing, China. That very modern press has also produced more than ten million copies of the Bible in Chinese. The attractive Bibles both in Chinese and ethnic minority languages sell for the equivalent of $1.50 in US currency.

For several years now, Akha Christian leaders from China, Burma and Thailand have been working to develop a "Universal Akha" translation of the New Testament. This means that they will try to find Akha terms understood by Akhas in all countries, even though modern terms, like the names of diseases or machinery, would be different for Akhas borrowing terms from Chinese or Thai or Burmese, depending on the area where they lived.

When that revised Akha New Testament can be printed, the hope is it can be printed by the Amity Press as well.

To us it seemed like Paul absorbed new languages effortlessly, a talent soon shared by our own children as they grew (and played with Lahu neighbors in

Kengtung.) Paul was soon talking to our kids in Lahu, sharing songs, translating for us parents who still struggled with the Shan language spoken in town.

Paul and I once gave a ride to some Akha teenagers who were singing loudly among themselves in the back of his pickup truck. "That's an interesting song," said Paul, and translated for me,

> "Young men should always wear plenty of flowers,
>
> Then their arms won't smell so bad . . . . "

He often had interesting anecdotes about local beliefs as well. Some people believed he kept a 'beeloo', an evil spirit, locked in the garage behind his house. "They tell each other it eats visitors who come to the house, and then passes silver coins in its droppings." This was easier for hill people to believe than that these white foreigners received a piece of mere paper each month and exchanged it for money down in Kengtung town. Paul assured us that Lois and I escaped this rumor because our garage had open slats in the doors, and people could see for themselves that we kept no such monster.

Paul and Elaine had no children, and at their next home furlough in the USA (one year out of every six, for advanced study, speaking in churches, and time with families), they applied to adopt two young boys. They designated us as character references, and we were able to truthfully tell the adoption board that whenever Paul and Elaine came down for a visit, our children always waited by the road at least two hours ahead of the time the Lewises could possibly arrive. The board took that as a very favorable reference. The Lewises returned with Bobby and Warren before we ourselves came due for home leave, and we came to know each other very well.

The military dictatorship took control of the national government in 1962, just before we left on home leave, and we were the first family to be denied re-entry a year later. Other foreigners soon followed and by 1965 almost all non-citizens were out of Burma. Several of us ex-Burma families were re-deployed to Thailand, the Lewises and us among them. The Lewises continued work among the Lahu and Akha living in northern Thailand; we began a new medical project among the Karen tribes farther south.

Paul earned a PhD degree in medical anthropology during home-leave; he and Elaine also published an illustrated book on the six major hill tribes in Thailand, called *Peoples of the Golden Triangle*. As they had done in Burma, they continued to publish various books in Lahu and Akha, such as a Lahu to English, English to Lahu dictionary, an Akha to English, English to Akha dictionary, along with health books, books of proverbs, etc.

Paul has helped the Lahu and Akha tribes, which number in the tens of thousands, to understand and cope with the 21st century. In their native hilltop territory, they have some advantages; living at a high enough altitude to escape the malaria mosquito and some of the other tropical diseases. The Akha also seem to have a natural immunity to leprosy ("because we eat dog meat," they explain.) When given the advantages of health and education, the Lahu and Akha are equal to anyone else. Sala Ai Pun, the former Lahu school principal, has eight adult children, each with a college degree. His daughter, Angela Pun, is on the faculty of the Myanmar Institute of Theology near Rangoon, and has visited USA twice as a missionary to the Americans, one of the pioneers in Asia-to-America missionary exchange.

There is no need to question the faith of these Asians; it exceeds that of many American Christians. Paul tells me (in 2015) that the Pangwai School is now Pangwai Seminary, offering three career tracks: social worker, rural school teacher (grades 1-6), and Master of Divinity Degree. Currently, 186 students are enrolled. And five Lahu men are now representatives (out of about 450) in Myanmar's National Parliament.

During their last few years of serving in Thailand, Paul and Elaine became aware of a problem they had not encountered before. Brothels in Thailand were proliferating at a rapid rate, sending agents to mountain villages to recruit young women for "jobs in the cities." Often girls from the hills saw this as an opportunity to aid their parents' income, but instead found themselves forced to become sex slaves in the houses of prostitution in Bangkok or other cities and towns in Thailand. In addition to the abusive treatment they had to endure, most became victims of HIV and other venereal diseases.

Paul and Elaine pioneered in establishing the "New Life Center" in Chiang Mai where tribal women with little or no education could live and study in night school. (There is also a branch in Chiang Rai. Both centers have "safe houses" to shelter those in imminent danger.)

With the help of a special police division in Bangkok, Paul and Elaine started a program of rescuing as many tribal girls out of the brothels as possible. This became the basis for world-wide efforts against human trafficking under the leadership of Lauren Bethell (see her chapter in this book.)

Paul told me that a few years ago, both Lahu and Akha friends warned him and his wife that brothel owners planned to kill them, because when the Lewises rescued girls out of sexual slavery their "owners" received no money from their "investment". Undaunted, Elaine turned to Paul and said, "If I have to give my life to save some girls from sex slavery, what a great way to go!"

Chapter 14

THE LANDGRAFS AND RONZHEIMERS: MARRIAGE REPAIR

Dr. John Landgraf was director of career counseling at The Center for Ministry when I and my family saw him as clients. We volunteered for reinstatement as medical missionaries to Thailand after a ten-year period of family medicine practice in USA. American Baptist Churches/USA wisely asks for examination after a several-year gap in someone's service, to see if a candidate really wants to work overseas, or is escaping some situation in America. Dr. Landgraf did that for several church groups, in addition to his usual clientele.

Three of our four children were in college or beyond; only fourteen-year-old Nancy was still at home. Nancy had some opinions of her own about being uprooted from all her friends and going back to a country she barely remembered.

"You're going to see a *shrink*? How come nobody

asks me to see the shrink? I'm going halfway around the world too!"

"I'll ask," I said.

"It's not routine, but sure, we can do it. Bring her along," the doctor said. The three of us took a three-day series of tests that dealt with our personalities and emotions at his Oakland, California office.

In the final interview, he asked about our plans for Nancy's schooling overseas.

"There's a branch of the International School in Chiang Mai she can attend while Lois and I are there for three months of language study. After that, she'll live in the student hostel in Bangkok," we explained.

He responded, "I suggest that you parents do your three months of language study in Bangkok. That way she'll only have to get used to one new school and group of friends. And Mrs. Dahlberg, I have a question for you: Why is it that every time I ask you something, you turn to look at your husband?"

We passed muster for the Mission, but took his counsel seriously. By the time we left for our duty station up north, three months later, Nancy had lived with us in Bangkok, was self-confident in riding the city buses or bargaining with a taxi driver, and she had found a Thai ballet teacher to continue the lessons she had been taking in USA. She made life-long friends among the other kids at the hostel, and two years later, in her junior year of high school, she became the first non-senior ever to be elected president of the 1,100-member student body of Bangkok's International School.

And Lois? Neither she nor I had noticed she always turned her head to me for answers. But now we try to share most decision-making equally. And it works.

Getting back to the Landgrafs. We discovered them now living in retirement in Idaho only forty miles from us, combining their skills to provide family counseling. We recently met them for lunch in Coeur d'Alene to catch up with each others' lives in the past thirty-eight years. Like many folks in the latter part of life, they are finding fulfillment in a new career related to their previous jobs—helping couples whose marriage is in difficulty from whatever cause. Further, Laura has launched an additional career as an author, activist and speaker on overcoming child abuse and related themes (www.lauralandgraf.com). As to their retreats (www.landgrafretreats.com), John and Laura's unique model is to take one couple at a time on retreat, concentrating on the couple's spousal relationship. Large group marriage enrichment retreats do that too, but not with two therapists for each couple. With laser-like focus, the Landgrafs hone in on every dynamic or goal the couple brings to the encounter, from making a good marriage even better to re-engineering the marriage for the empty nest or retirement years, or in helping a couple take their marriage apart if one or both partners are unwilling to reinvent their marriage with new vows. Dr.

Landgraf has been known to cite the Confederate Cavalry Manual printed in 1861: "If your horse gets shot and dies, dismount."

Laura, the eldest child of missionary parents, was born in Oregon, but reared in Ethiopia, and still can speak the Amharic language. She returned to America to attend college, and chose to stay. In addition to a shared interest in music (the Landgrafs have several CDs to their credit) she has lately developed a specialty of dealing with marriages in which the wife suffered abuse as a child, an increasingly frequent situation, which can have profound but often unrecognized effects in that child's marriage during her adulthood. She deals with this more recent specialty and related themes in her blog (see above.)

This is a good point at which to introduce another counselor, whom I met when I attended a writer's conference in 2007. Dr. Bill Ronzheimer and his wife were just beginning a book about marriages in which the wife has suffered sexual abuse in childhood. Bill has developed the subject from the standpoint of husbands who may not even know about the wife's abuse as a child, until some event triggers an unexpected emotional attitude that endangers the marriage.

His Marriage Reconstruction blog is worthwhile reading. (www.marriagreconstructiom.com) A good place to start might be his 22nd July, 2015 post:

"How to respond when childhood sexual abuse [of a wife] is disclosed." There are responses by the husband that are helpful, and others which are best avoided. Anger against the perpetrator (for example) is understandable but, twenty to thirty years after the fact, may be counter-productive.

Like most family medicine practitioners, I have encountered marriages in various stages and causes of distress, but I don't consider myself qualified to handle such cases. Teams like the Landgrafs and/or the Ronzheimers, however, appear to be competent and caring examples of those who bring healing and hope for marriages that are not the joyful fulfillment of life that they could be.

Chapter 15

MASS-RESPONSE: COUNTERING
GENOCIDE IN CAMBODIA

In 1979, Communist Viet Nam invaded Communist
Cambodia, where Pol Pot had set up his Khmer
Rouge government. The Khmer Rouge are said to
have executed between one and two million of their
own citizens during Pol Pot's doctrinaire rule. During
rainy season, the mud kept the two armies apart. But
in late October, the Vietnamese tanks could move
across the land again, pinning the Khmer Rouge
army against the Thai border.

Each army had tried to deny food to the other, and
so each side had destroyed crops wherever they
found them. Hundreds of thousands of Cambodian
refugees, mixed with fleeing Khmer Rouge soldiers,
were caught in the hill forests of western Cambodia.
They had no food except leaves on the trees, and no
protection from malaria and other forest diseases. As
the Vietnamese army drew closer, a half-million or

more sick and starving humans fled across the border into Thailand.

There was nowhere to put them. The daily newspapers carried pictures of dying children and mass burials. Thirty-thousand refugees flooded across the border in a single day, near the border town of Aranyaprathet, and were vulnerable to the mortar shells of the pursuing Vietnamese. The Thai army assembled dozens of buses to move the refugees away from the border, and set up the first of many camps by clearing a field near the town of Sa Kaew.

Up in Mae Sariang, 500 miles to the northwest, I wrote to our former neighbors Bob and Pat Coats who now worked at mission headquarters in Bangkok.

"We understand that some 91,000 have come across the border from Cambodia, and that medical workers are swamped. We try to look at this realistically and not let our emotions run away with us. But the thought persists that here we are, in our slack season, [during rice harvest] seeing patients for only 3 to 5 hours a day. We could spare one doctor for a month if you can use us. We don't know if this is God's will or not, but thought we would make the offer and see what He does with it."

A telegram arrived asking us to come as soon as possible. Lois and I were in the first group to go, along with nurse Rosa Crespo-Harris, Mala (a Karen nurse) and Weena, a (Karen nurse-aide). We drove to

Chiang Mai next day and took the overnight train to Bangkok, where Bob and Pat Coats met us. They explained that we would be on loan to CAMA Services, the relief arm of the Christian and Missionary Alliance Church. We would work at the Sa Kaew camp, a three hour drive east of Bangkok, where Red Cross was setting up a tent hospital. CAMA had a permanent medical team coming from Holland, but they wouldn't arrive for two weeks. Rescue workers said thousands more refugees were scattered about the border area, many of them too weak to walk. Sa Kaew camp was four days old when we arrived, andhad 30,000 refugees, 1,200 of them in the make-shift camp hospital. Some ill Communist soldiers were among them, but those strong enough to fight were still across the border in Cambodia.

Our driver turned off the highway and stopped at a Thai Army checkpoint, where a Red Cross worker gave us ID cards. My first impressions were of a sea of mud, surrounded by barbed wire. Thousands of make-shift lean-tos (blue plastic sheets, each supported by a few sticks) crowded the fields. Our first problem was to navigate the deep mud. We picked our way from rock to tree root; at one point, Lois had to reach elbow-deep into the mud to retrieve a shoe. The hospital area was on slightly higher, more solid ground.

The refugees were deathly afraid of the Khmer Rouge soldiers among them, and we had no way of telling who was who. We just treated them all as the severely ill humans they were. We didn't even have a translator for the first few days.

That first day was chaos. We were put to work immediately upon arrival, I with another new doctor, Lois over in a large tent full of orphan children. We lost track of the other team members. None of us knew where things were, or even what was available. Each of us scrounged through the supply tents to find whatever might be useful. At dusk, another convoy of Thai army trucks arrived, bearing more starved, feverish, even unconscious people, everyone dressed in black, with meager bundles of cook pots or other small possessions. Some made no move to get down from the truck, so workers clambered up to pass them down to those of us waiting on the ground. Another worker and I struggled to carry a comatose man on a piece of cardboard over to the perimeter fence and pass him through the barbwire to others inside.

Many of these people had lived off nothing but their own body tissues for weeks, and had arms and legs scarcely bigger around than their skin-covered bones. They had lost all fat and most of their muscle to fuel the remaining small spark of life. Even the proteins to make digestive juices were gone.

We had to be very careful not to overload their digestive systems those first few days. We started with clear broth, with a little rice and vegetables mixed in. Some couldn't even handle that, and quietly died after reaching the camp. After a day or two, we added protein gruel—"Kaset food"—made by Kasetsart University in Bangkok. Weena carried a pail of it back and forth, ladling out a cup twice a day to each of our ward's hundred and fifty patients. Later still, rice and curry came from a central kitchen for all 30,000 now in the camp. Different volunteer groups managed each of the dozen or so tent-wards; we cooperated with each other, but we were too fatigued to socialize much.

We treated malaria, diarrhea, pneumonia, parasitic worms, anemia, and nutritional deficiencies. The chief deficiencies were iron (malaria destroys red blood cells) and beri-beri (lack of thiamine, one of the B vitamins, causing nerve weakness and heart failure.) That first day, we had nothing to clean patients with, nor any change of clothing for those who had soiled themselves. Each morning when we came to work, those who had died in the night were outside the tent, rolled up in their bamboo mats. We took the dead to the penetrating stench of the morgue tent at the far edge of the hospital area, to await burial in mass graves by Buddhist monks who volunteered their service.

Those first few days, silence reigned in the hospital tents except for coughing. Not even a baby crying. Everyone lay there on mats, too weak to move. I remember how, during the first week, they gradually began to talk and even smile and walk around as they grew stronger. In particular I remember two men, an amputee and a blind man, who often walked together, the cripple on his crutches, holding a guide-stick for his blind friend to grasp and follow.

Daily bus-loads of volunteers swarmed out from Bangkok to respond to the need. Leaders of Bangkok society mingled with students, digging ditches, feeding patients, acting as go-fers. Our daughter Nancy and some of her schoolmates from International High School used their "Senior Sneak" holiday to come help. One elderly European man, with whom I could only converse in Thai, adopted an old Cambodian who was too weak to lift a spoon by himself, and stayed with him night and day until the old man died.

Bob Jono, a CAMA supervisor, saw to the medical team's needs. He found us a Khmer man who spoke Thai, and a Khmer girl who had returned from her home in New Zealand to help her fellow Cambodians, despite her terror that the Khmer Rouge would murder her. That made our job much easier. Through an interpreter, we could hear the patient's symptoms; we no longer had to practice "veterinary medicine."

Jono and his crew also made sure that a hot meal awaited us back at our house in town each night. The camp had a security curfew, not even medics were allowed to stay after dark, except for a single team to keep watch over the whole 1000-bed hospital from six p.m. until eight a.m. Jono and I had to stay after the rest of the team left, for a staff meeting at the Red Cross tent each evening, where the day's problems were worked out. I got back to town each night about

7:30 p.m. after a thirteen-hour day, ate supper, and fell into bed.

The second week was a little better. Fewer died, and many were obviously recovering. A lab technician appeared from somewhere, and set up a blood transfusion service. He split every pint in two; even a half pint is enough to help someone with a hematocrit of only two (normal 12-16.) By mutual consent, the medical teams refused news interviews unless the reporter could show his receipt for having donated blood.

An orphan girl in our tent, eight or ten years old, pointed excitedly one morning at the passing people. Her father and sister had just passed by; she had been separated from them a year ago! And a little girl who had been bed-ridden with beri-beri heart disease squealed in mock alarm as her sister told her I was coming to give her a shot. (I wasn't.)

Lois and I had even taken our turn on the all-night hospital crew. There isn't much you can do for a thousand patients, most of whom you've never seen before. Four of us (our translator, a new nurse, Ruth Jones, and Lois and I) tried to visit every ward at least every three hours and be sure the IVs were running properly. We removed two patients who had died; checked one teenage boy with severe diarrhea, and a couple of women in labor.

About three o'clock in the morning, I took a few minutes break to chat with the Israeli military doctor from the triage tent, the only other medic who was allowed to stay all night. We watched a team of workers adjust the new lighting on a scaffold outside, where a drilling crew was sinking a well. As we looked up at the scaffold, I said meditatively, "Haman built a gallows, fifty cubits high . . ."

Startled, the Israeli demanded, "How did you know what I was thinking! Where did you hear that story?"

"Hey, the book of Esther is in our scriptures too, just like yours."

News media were everywhere, every day. A man squatted beside me with a handheld microphone as I treated a boy for pneumonia, and asked me to describe the case. I am told I was on Voice of America Radio the next night. A few days later, a television crew from NBC taped the hospital. I happened to be the only doctor available who had an American accent. Letters from back home later told me I had appeared in all the bars in Kellogg, to shouts of "Hey! There's Doc Dahlberg on TV!" The broadcast was repeated several times all over USA and Europe, probably the only time in my life I will ever speak to over a hundred million people. At the time, I was more concerned with hiding my feet so the camera wouldn't show how swollen my legs were from long hours without rest.

Rosalynn Carter talked with Lois when the First Lady toured the camp. (I missed that because I was at a meeting back in town that day, orienting a group of newly arrived doctors.) Mrs. Carter asked her several questions, but Lois says her own finest moment was in response to all the newsmen, who nearly trampled our patients as they shouted at her, "Get down! Get down!" so they could get a clear photo of the President's wife. Lois said, "If the reporters would move back a few feet, they wouldn't be standing in the patients' latrine ditch." A lady in the group said, "Oh dear! I wish I'd known that a little sooner." And one of Mrs. Carter's Secret Service men grinned to Lois, "Say it louder. We're being recorded."

We were more tired every day than I can ever remember being. And I felt a dull anger as I watched some of my patients die, anonymous and alone; an anger at those who start wars and let others pay the consequences. But you suppress your emotions after the first day or two, because you have to choose between emoting about the tragedy, or doing something to fix it. I found I don't have enough personal resources to do both.

We left our ward in the hands of a Dutch lady, Eva Hartog, a TV personality who brought a team of eight Dutch nurses to work with the doctors who would inherit our tent. The day we left, most of the refugees were visiting back and forth. Kids were playing games, or standing in line for milk, wearing their tin bowls on their heads as pretend helmets. It's good to know we made a difference.

But the feeling I remember most, and am most grateful for, came to me one evening after the nightly staff meeting, as I drove back to town alone in the warm night air. Through the open car window I inhaled the pungent, vinegar smell of the tapioca crop drying in the farmyards I passed. I felt at peace, tired but no longer drooping with fatigue. We had taken everything that Sa Kaew camp had thrown at us, and most of our patients were getting well. And I thought, I can do this! I can practice medicine under the worst conditions, and still look anyone in the eye and know without any doubt: *I am a doctor.* No one can ever take that away from me.

And I shall always remember the effect a single letter or action can have on one's life when mailed at the right moment, effect not only on other people's lives, but on my own.

The third group of chapters are about unexpected, highly unlikely encounters; each of which I witnessed. I am a skeptic by inclination, with a background in chemistry and medicine. I am not trained in statistics, but I do have a son-in-law who is a mathematician with some thirty years professional experience, and who is even more skeptical than I. When I asked his opinion on causation by random chance, he said that chances of any one event like these in one's lifetime would be quite reasonable; perhaps two might happen. But five or six? He couldn't say. I suspect random chance alone would be less likely than the traditional cliche of "one-in-a-million", unless other factors played a part.

Chapter 16

PETER DORAN: TAXI DRIVER, SAMARITAN

It was 1947, I was 18, and hitch-hiking from my summer job in Green Lake, Wisconsin, home to Syracuse, New York. I wanted to see more of the USA and Canada, and collect minerals for my collection, along the way.

I had been through Sault Ste. Marie and Sudbury, Ontario the previous year and now I aimed to go north of Lake Superior along the only existing road across Canada at that time. It included a three-hundred mile stretch of two-lane gravel road through mostly uninhabited wilderness. The present section of theTrans-Canada Highway between Nipigon and Sault Ste. Marie had not yet been completed.

The trip was fine through St. Paul and Duluth, until I reached the Canadian entry point at Pigeon River, Ontario. The Canadian immigration officer had been watching me as I walked across the bridge. He stopped me. "Why are you entering Canada? Who are you planning to visit? What's his address and occupation? Bad country up there in the bush. Got food with you? How much money? Let's see it." Only a written invitation from a doctor/rock-hound, and the thirty-nine dollars in my wallet allayed his doubts about my survival "up in the bush." He gave me a note to hand in at Niagara Falls, Ontario, so they could search for my carcass if the note hadn't been turned in within eight days.

I continued on to Fort William, now part of Thunder Bay, and went mineral hunting with my contact there, Dr. Peter Wenger. He and his family and I dug excellent specimens of amethyst crystals at the end of a little dirt road. I continued on the next day to Nipigon, a timber and tourist center some eighty miles further northeast. From there onward, I encountered problems.

Trouble was, Canadian hitchhikers with insufficient funds were turned back by US Immigration, just as I had almost been by the Canadian officer. Only one road lay ahead, with no bus service, and few cars driving very far. Most travelers went by train or plane, or drove south of Lake Superior through the US. At some points, there were three or four hitch-hikers waiting for rides. I managed only one hundred miles the whole day, ending up in the small lumber and mining town of Geraldton, which was celebrating its tenth year of existence that week. After waiting hours at the highway junction, I searched for shelter from the evening cold. The only hotel wanted ten dollars a night. My shrinking supply of cash wouldn't last long at that rate. The desk clerk disdainfully referred me to a place called the Colonial Rooms, which charged two dollars. It was a real dump, noisy, dirty, with a non-functioningwater supply. I locked my room door.

Up before dawn the next day, I got a ride two miles to the highway junction with a couple of men on their way to work. Two hikers were already there. The sunrise was spectacular, but the wind bitterly cold. The pair of hikers accepted a ride going to Longlac, twenty miles east, but I resolved to only ride with someone going as far as Hearst, the other side of the 140 mile totally uninhabited stretch. But after a couple hours of freezing, I rode the local bus back into town to check the train schedule. The station was open but not the ticket window yet, so I found a shop open and got breakfast. Back at the station, the daily train east would cost seventeen dollars, and involve three transfers totaling thirty-six hours to reach Toronto.

I was supposed to meet my friend Ambrose Smith the next day in the town of Cobalt, still more than 400 miles away. That would have to be abandoned if I took the train. It would come in about an hour. I warmed myself in the station and thought about it; finally felt strong enough and warm enough to go back to the highway junction and try again. After another two hours, I finally caught a ride to Longlac, twenty miles east. The two hikers I had met earlier were still there. They planned to hop a freight train, but finally started walking east. It was warmer in the sun now; I bought a small bag of peanuts for lunch, and avoided eye contact with a highway patrol car at the gas station.

At noon—24 hours without significant progress—I gave up. I was beaten. And then, strangely, I felt fine; no more worry, everything seemed okay. If there was no ride by 3 p.m I would start gathering kindling and wood for a fire, and sleep under the small bridge at Longlac, taking tomorrow's train to North Bay (not far from Cobalt.) I would wire Amby to meet me there.

About 2:30, a car approached. I raised my thumb, then lowered it in disgust as I saw the sign TAXI. It swept by me, then screeched to a stop fifty yards away. I jogged up to it and asked, "Are you going as far as Hearst, sir?"

"Yuh."

Oboy! I raced back to grab my bag at the bridge.

"Let's go, buddy, I'm in a hurry!" the driver said.

"So am I, sir!"

He grinned and told me to throw my bag in the back. Asked me where I was going.

"Cobalt." I saw him half-grin again.

"You aren't going there are you!"

"Darn near."

And everything was fine again. He was headed for

Kirkland Lake, only seventy miles from Cobalt, and had to be there tonight. We passed the two hikers by the side of the road; I suggested they needed a ride, too. He looked annoyed, said one rider was enough; he'd never risk picking up a pair.

We sped along the dusty road, making good time. But ten miles beyond Longlac we came to a road grading crew, and there at the side of the road were three forlorn hikers. When I remarked in surprise that they had passed me two days ago, only 150 miles back, he ground to a stop, swearing. "I can't leave them in the middle of nowhere. You say you know them?"

Fearful of robbery.

"I've seen them along the road a couple of times. One's bound for Ottawa, and the other two for Toronto, I think."

"#&*! Now we can't make good time with the back end loaded that way!" As the three ran up, panting for breath, the driver was clearly unwelcoming. But no hiker would have enough pride to turn down a ride after being stranded two days. The five of us sped on, averaging 61 mph in spite of the extra load, the ruts, and the dust. We crossed large north-bound rivers, the Pagwachuan, the Nagagami, the Kabinakagami. No houses, no signs except a marker every 10 miles. The driver stopped occasionally to add a quart of oil to the engine, or to pump up a soft tire from a cartridge of CO_2. Finally we reached Hearst and stopped for gas. The driver opened the back door. "I picked you fellas up because you were foolish enough to get stuck way out in the woods. Now you're in a town again, and you'll have to get out." He turned to me. "You can stay." The three looked stunned, but they were over the worst part. I was grateful for my good fortune; ashamed too. Given a choice, I'm sure I wouldn't have given up my favored position willingly.

The road was potholed and terrible. We stopped at a little place called Mattice to get a front tire fixed at a garage. While waiting, we got a sandwich and coffee. He waved away my money, saying he'd take care of it. We talked occasionally as we continued on. I told him about collecting minerals, and about college in Syracuse. He owned a gas station between Schreiber and Nipigon. and often ran his taxi between there and Kirkland Lake for those willing to pay the price; faster than train, cheaper than plane. He had a number of stories to tell, mainly about passengers he had carried. His wife was in Kirkland now, but was taking an 11 p.m. train and he wanted to be there in time to see her off.

We passed Kapuskasing and its airport. It was getting dark, and we had to slow to 45 or 50. The dimmer switch on his headlights didn't work, and after hitting one large bump, the lights went off entirely. He stopped quickly. When the lights came on again, we were pointed toward the ditch. All the garages in Cochrane were closed. We stopped for gas and got coffee and hamburgers, for which I paid this time. At one point we came across a family with a car

108

stalled on the railroad tracks. We pushed them a little ways, but their car wouldn't start. My driver (Peter Doran, I had learned by now) lifted the hood and soon fixed the trouble, refusing any payment.

Nearing Kirkland, we reached pavement again, a big relief. We were in tourist country now. We reached the town at 11:30 p.m. Eastern time, and I guess he missed his wife's train. He bid me goodbye outside a hotel (same price as the hole-in-the-wall in Geraldton, but much better), gave me his address and told me to drop him a line sometime. I did, but never got a reply.

I met my friend Ambrose about noon the next day in Cobalt. We did find some mineral specimens there, and the rest of the trip, through North Bay, Toronto, and Niagara Falls was uneventful.

But I thank God, for sending Peter Doran and his taxi (God's sense of humor, that?)

Updating this memoir for my book, I put Peter Doran's name on the Internet and promptly found his widow's obituary. She had died in April, 2014, three months short of age 100. The announcement listed family survivors. I wrote the funeral home, explaining my reason for writing and asked that they forward my letter to Peter's son Patrick. A couple weeks later, he phoned me from Kapuskasing, Ontario.

He confirmed his father's management of a gas

station in Rossport and later in Schreiber. He (Pat) would have been a child back in 1947 and may have been with his mother that night she took the train, but he can't remember their destination. He gave a brief account of his father's work history: first a miner in the Kirkland Lake area, then operated three trucks that took part in the construction of the Hearst/Longlac section of the highway, during World War II. Canada was desperately trying to complete this last section of road connection between the eastern and western parts of the country to supplement their transcontinental railroad.

Peter was in his thirties when he moved his family to the Schreiber/Terrace Bay area of Ontario, opening a gas station, and then a larger station, and his taxi service between Schreiber, Kirkland Lake, and Thunder Bay, and finally a prominent car dealership.

Around 1955 Peter developed lung cancer, probably related to "getting dusted" (silicosis) in his mining years, resulting in lung surgery and finally his death in 1960. It's not surprising, then, that he failed to respond to my postcard from Thonze, Burma, in the summer of 1957, ten years after my ride with him.

His son Pat did not choose to take over the family business, but became a high school teacher and married a pharmacist; a marriage now in its 51st year. His wife serves on the Kapuskasing Library Board. He says that my account of his father is not unique. Over the years, several other people have told him of things his father did for them.

I myself worked as a taxi driver in Syracuse during part of my time in medical school. But I have never known a driver who, on a single trip, rescued four hitchhikers, and repaired a car stalled on the railroad tracks, all without taking any payment. Peter Doran taught me that any job has opportunities to be a good Samaritan.

Chapter 17

BILL W. HARMON: THE ONLY POSSIBLE DAY

In the summer of 1992, Lois and I drove east to visit our daughter Pat at Fort Leonard Wood in Missouri, and then went on to visit other relatives and friends in eastern USA. On our return trip we took a more northern route, through my early childhood city of St. Paul, Minnesota. I thought I could show my wife all three houses my family had lived in during the time when I was two to ten years old.

We began our exploration in mid-morning, searching out 1025 Goodrich Ave. and when we found it Lois took immediate interest: "Look! The sign says Estate Sale. That means we can go inside and look around!" And we did. Other people were going in and out as well. I couldn't recognize much —I was only four years old back then—but the basement brought to memory our old washer and wringer, and the time the fire engines came when the ironing board caught fire in the night.

After we had gone through all the rooms, I told the lady at the front door that I used to live in this house, and asked who owned it now. She indicated a man out on the sidewalk. "That's the brother of the man who died; he's just come up from Chicago for the day; he'd probably like to talk with you." I went out and shook hands with a man about my own age, Bill Harmon, and asked how long his family had lived here.

He said he had lived there in childhood, and thought his father had bought the house from a minister. "That would be my Dad," I said. We talked awhile, and as Lois and I were leaving, he asked, "Where you from?"

"Kellogg, Idaho."

His jaw dropped. "I can't believe this," he said, my family owns a mine near Kellogg!"

That extended our conversation, of course. His father and uncle, both graduates in mining at the U of Minnesota in 1915 – 1917; had been prospectors in the 1930s. They had established a small mine, The Northern Light, that had produced lead and silver for a few years during the war, and closed in 1950. He mentioned a law firm I recognized, and I said I would try and locate his mine and send him some pictures. "What are the odds," we asked each other, "of our both being here on the single day we are both in town?" And moreover, each having work interests in another small town 1,400 miles distant from our present meeting place?

Bill and I have corresponded occasionally since then; I located the mine — a couple of short tunnels near Pine Creek Road, two miles from my office in Pinehurst, Idaho. He wrote that he had convinced his family to hold their next year's reunion in Idaho's Silver Valley. Unfortunately, that was the year, 1993, when I was already signed up to do nine-months at Kwai River Hospital in Thailand, so I missed his family reunion.

In the twenty-three years since that meeting, each of us has become an author. He had a great-uncle in the Diplomatic Service who had retired in Malaga, Spain just before the Spanish Civil War began in 1936. He had left daily diaries which Bill collected and published, *Death in Malaga, an American Eye Witness*, giving a vivid picture of Franco's Spanish dictatorship of that time, and the reactions of both Spaniards and the few Americans who stayed during the war. That localized conflict became the testing ground for Hitler's air force and tanks as Germany prepared to overrun Europe and North Africa three years later in 1940.

Now retired, Bill Harmon travels the world widely, observing and writing details which might escape the notice of most one-time tourists abroad. Hopefully, he may have other stories to write. It hadn't occurred to me to ask about Bill's daytime job until recently. Turns out he had a fifty-one-year career in the Leo Burnett Company, one of the largest marketing firms in the world.

Without a job when he was discharged from the army in 1951, he had a blind date with a girl who worked for a top executive in that company. She got him a night job in the mail room serving the company's sixteen-story office building. He met Leo Burnett in person one night. While Bill was running the Pitney Bowes stamping machine, "this short, big-lipped, balding man" appeared and said there was a letter in the pile that *must not* go out. Bill invited him to dig into the pile. Bill's boss showed up soon after, told Bill that's Mr. Burnett, the company president, and they all three dove into the pile. It was Bill who found the letter. Burnett turned to Bill and said, "You are the type of person we want at our company!"

Bill rose through the ranks in the media division, dealing with a variety of clients around the world; cigarette, food, deodorant, soap accounts, beer, cars, insurance, each spending up to a hundred million dollars annually, "and many I chose to forget," he said. In the computer age he worked with purchasing lists of special audiences supplied by Google. He also taught media advertising at Northwestern University in Chicago.

In an industry traditionally associated with hype and high pressure, Leo Burnett Company or one of its world branches won the International Andy Award six consecutive years. This is a distinction reportedly upholding the standards of craftsmanship, creativity, and taste. It has to be said, standards could be even higher in media advertising, but still there is hope.

Chapter 18

JOHN THARP, MIKE and LORA BORDEN:
Two Cases: The Only Possible Hour.

After closing my office medical practice in Pinehurst, Idaho in 1993, I spent the next eleven years as a part-time *locum tenens* ("rent-a-doc") traveling to fill temporary vacancies in doctors' offices or hospital emergency rooms. It's an ideal job for semi-retirement. Although I had to thoroughly document and update my resumé for the medical employment agency, the agency matched me to jobs available as often or as rarely as I wished to work, usually anywhere from a weekend to a month or more, several times a year.

About half the states in America had reciprocity agreements with the Idaho State Board of Medicine, so getting a temporary medical license in any of those states was not hard to arrange. The agency paid motel and travel expenses, licensing and malpractice insurance fees, and a pay scale that was quite acceptable, considering I would not have to pay nurse's salaries or office expenses. The income from these trips, several each year, also funded trips for further volunteer work overseas.

In 1999, I worked several weeks in St. Francis, Kansas, a small town far up in the northwest corner of the state, just across the border from Colorado and Nebraska. On my first trip there, I noted one clinic patient's name was Slusher, and remarked that that was a common name in my home town of Kellogg, Idaho, a thousand miles from Kansas. He smiled and said yes, he used to be my patient up there a few years back. This was not all that remarkable, but it did wonders for my reputation with the clinic nurses, who assumed that one of my patients "traveled all the way from Idaho to consult me."

St. Francis is a pleasant little town in the semi-desert of America's high plains. The hospital took good care of me, providing free lodging in a home whose owner was away on vacation. I later moved to a motel out on highway 36. I was up early next morning, searching for some place to eat. The motel restaurant wasn't open yet, but I could see a gas station a quarter-mile down the highway, and figured I could at least find coffee there, so I started walking toward it.

Midway, I met a man of about age 50 coming toward me with a cup of coffee. He stopped and said, "I know you! We were at board meetings together in Philadelphia!" He was staying at the motel, traveling by bicycle from Utah to Illinois. We had served together on the American Baptist Foreign Mission Board several years before, but had no contact since then.

I know New Yorkers boast that, if you stand at Times Square long enough, you will see someone you know from back home. But in a town of 1,300 on a two-lane road where Kansas, Nebraska and Colorado meet? What are the chances for the one morning that two acquaintances, one from Idaho and one from Illinois, are in town and will walk into each other along the shoulder of one of the back roads of Kansas?

John Tharp and I had breakfast together, and later that morning he rode his bicycle in to town to see the hospital where I was working, before continuing his journey eastward.

I have occasionally wondered, in the ensuing fifteen years, whether God had a purpose in that meeting. I have not perceived any reason in my own life, and finally I wrote John to see if he was aware of any in his.

He replied that he, too, remembered the incident and had wondered about a reason. He had not detected any, but said that after a number of such coincidences in his life, it has often entered his mind that this may be a way that God alerts us to possibilities, to keep us ready for the occasional time when He does indeed want action from us.

So far, this story may be relevant to coincidences, but not to this book's theme of achieving great goals. Here is a sequel that came to my attention in the week (in 2015) that I was writing this. The couple telling it used to be patients of mine in Idaho, some twenty years ago. The family has been overseas in India most of the intervening years, and plan to return there this Fall. Mike Bordon tells this story (with minor editing):

On July 1, 2015, (Mike writes) my wife Lora and I were driving west on I-94 approaching Bismarck, North Dakota. We decided to stop in Bismarck and have dinner. We planned to drive further west to Dickinson and spend the night there afterward.

As we exited the freeway at Bismarck we saw signs for the various restaurants that were available at that location. Lora's eyes immediately caught sight of a Chinese place that featured a Mongolian barbecue. We both like Asian food. Lora loves it. She mentioned that option. I replied, "That sounds great to me." I thought it was decided.

As we approached the turning lane, Lora then said, "There's a Perkins. Let's try that." I was mildly surprised, knowing her likes and dislikes. So I took a right into the parking lot which put us in front of the Perkins entrance. Even as I was turning I still thought this is surprising. I hesitated briefly as I began to turn in, but she said definitely, "Let's go to Perkins."

We entered the restaurant and were seated at a

booth at the window. The window was blocked by an exterior advertising banner. We sat down and were handed our menus. Lora left for the ladies room.

As she did, I sat facing the corner of the dining room. Two empty tables away from us, right in the corner, sat a family. It appeared to be mom, dad, and four kids, starting with a blonde girl aged about 13, on downward. They were in mid-meal. Mom seemed to be talking to them, in a somewhat serious manner that made me think she was relating a story to them, or making a point to the whole family. I liked how she seemed to be relating to the kids.

hen I felt a surge of compassion for the family. I had a strong urge to pray for them right then and there. I silently prayed, still feeling this intense compassion. I prayed for their marriage, that it would be strong. Then I prayed for their relationship with the four children, that it would be blessed. As I finished these two short, sincere prayers, I had an impression that I was to tell them they were an awesome family. For whatever reason, I did not act on that.

Lora returned. I didn't say anything to her about what I'd felt. We talked about the menu.

The family was getting up as their meal ended, and mom and some of the kids left the table. Since I needed the restroom, I got up, and hoped to speak to the family on the way. I did see the blonde girl near the cash register. I thought of telling her "you guys are an awesome family," but I didn't. It seemed better to speak to one of the adults. I returned to our table without seeing either of them.

We decided we should change tables, as the banner totally blocked our view. We couldn't see the waitress. Lora said, "Let's do it." She got up and I followed, and she went to the window table right beside the family. As we sat down, only the dad and a young boy were still seated. Dinner was over and obviously they were just about to leave.

Once we were seated, the dad immediately said to us with a grin, "Do you want some free coffee?" He held up his pitcher. We laughed. As he and his son slid out of their booth and stood to go, he paused and talked about where they were going but included the phrase "We're missionaries."

I asked, "You are missionaries?"

"Yes, we serve in Russia, in the far eastern part of Russia."

Being lifetime missionaries ourselves, I told him, "We are missionaries too. We work with YWAM (Youth With A Mission).We served in India for many years and now work at one of our mission's training centers in Lebanon, Pennsylvania."

Dad (whose name was Steve) said, "Oh, my wife's uncle works with YWAM in Mongolia." As he finished that sentence, his voice trailed off as if he were trying to remember a name. He mumbled the word, "Simar."

Surprised at a familiar name, I said, "Do you mean

Byron and Sondra Simar?"

"Yes."

"We know them. They received training with us in Pennsylvania before they went to Mongolia. We had hoped to recruit them to work with us in the USA. But of course, we're thrilled that they ended up in Mongolia."

"We have been considering leaving our mission," Steve said, "we're looking into YWAM. In fact after we go to Seattle for my dad's surgery, we plan to go to Colorado Springs to talk to YWAM about possibilities."

I told Steve about my prayer for him and that feeling of compassion. After a little more conversation, Steve walked away toward the exit, and seconds later mom (Amanda) appeared. She said, "So I understand you guys know my Uncle Byron. They are a big reason why I am in missions. They have inspired me a lot."

"They are wonderful," Lora said. Then I told Amanda about how I'd felt deep emotion and had prayed for them.

I said, "You guys are truly an awesome family."

Amanda shyly put her arms around the 13 year old blonde girl's neck from behind, embraced her, smiled and said, "This really seems like God is doing something."

Being in amazement, we both replied, "Oh yes!"

We talked a little more. Then they went out into the parking lot, and as we watched, began to organize the mini-van and kids to continue their trip toward Seattle.

I was very excited. "Think of all the bits and pieces that had to come together for us to meet them here today," I said to Lora.

They had driven from Minnesota to Bismarck that day. We had driven from Green Bay to Bismarck with a lot of tourist stops on the way. We got to the restaurant about the same time. We oddly chose to eat at Perkins. Even though we were sitting two tables away from them, I had this strong impression to pray and to speak to them. Lora chose to move to the table beside them. Steve started a conversation. He mentioned being missionaries. He said the word "Simar." We work in the mission they are considering being a part of. I wondered how does God do that? How does he control all these circumstances? He moved two families, total strangers, together for a meeting and some words of encouragement. His power was working and guiding, but we only realized it after the fact.

As we ate our meal and watched them prepare to leave from the parking lot, the young boy ran over to our table and said, "My dad said to give this to you." It was a $25 Perkins gift card. Our meal ended up being about $20 and with the tip, it was covered. As they drove out, Steve leaned forward and waved, and I returned the wave, feeling a rush of emotion. We were pilgrims on a journey with God, spending some meaningful moments together.

"Lora," I said, "This morning, if I had told you someone would buy our meal tonight at Perkins in Bismarck, North Dakota, what would you have said?"

She replied, "No way, I'd have thought . . . impossible!"

Chapter 19

NURSES FOR THE HOSPITAL: The same moment

June, 1965: The town of Mae Sariang had been undergoing change for the past month, as the new all-weather highway approached. The two-lane asphalt pavement was still 45 miles away, but the bulldozers and graders had been busy only a block behind our house, filling a large ravine and smoothing the right of way through the brush, slowly proceeding toward the province capital of Mae Hong Son, one hundred miles to the north. Even though the beginning of rainy season would soon turn the town airstrip into deep mud until November, the town would now have access to the rest of the country.

Our outpatient clinic had been open since February, and our ten-bed hospital and operating room were now complete. But aside from occasional visits by student nurses from Chiang Mai, 130 miles away, we had only two nurses: Lois (part time) and Christabel, plus two or three aides with the equivalent of a middle school education. We were already beginning to see highway and construction accidents and occasional abdominal surgical cases which we could have done, with an operating room team, but had to refer in to Chiang Mai University Hospital, a four hour trip by taxi at best.

We had been inspected and approved by the Thai public health officials. The frequent orders from Immigration for me to leave the country stopped after a visit by the Mae Hong Son Assistant Governor, who was escorting a royal princess (probably Princess Galyani, King Bhumibol's sister) who wanted to tour the hospital. We had supplies, we had a lab/Xray tech who was learning rapidly, but we had only two nurses. The Princess asked, among other questions, "How many doctors do you have?"

I replied "Just one, and Immigration has ordered me to leave the country next week." the Asst. Governor was paying attention, and I soon received permission to stay the remaining two years of my term.

The three missionary families in Mae Sariang at the time (Don and Janet Schlatter of New Tribes, Bob and Pat Coats, and Lois and myself of the Northern Baptists) met together every week,

socially and for prayer. The nursing shortage affected the work of all of us, and one afternoon we took it to God in prayer, each of us around the small circle in turn. We all believed that we were attempting to do God's work, but we also realized that God often worked on a different schedule from ours.

Not this time. Before we had gone all the way around our circle, there was a thump on the porch. I went to the door; a taxi driver asked where we wanted some baggage put. Two Thai graduate nurse/midwives from McCormick Hospital in Chiang Mai stood behind him.

One we knew: Orawan had visited us for a few days in February, and was just back for an impromptu visit. The other, Yawaluk, stayed on with us, our first new full-time nurse. We had no idea they were coming at any time, let alone at that moment.

Two weeks later, a motorcycle pulled up with another nurse aboard; Gaysala was just looking us over then, but signed on three days later. That same day, two other nurses appeared, natives of Mae Sariang. They had been working up north in Mae Hong Son, but they wanted to work with us so they could live at home. A missionary nurse transferring from another country, Esther Greenmun, arrived in time to take a month of anesthesia training in Chiang Mai, before beginning work here. We were soon doing general surgery, including trauma, appendixes, Caesarian sections, occasional amputations and upper abdominal procedures.

As my Dad used to remark, "When people pray, coincidences happen more often."

Chapter 20

DAI WAN:
WHY DIDN'T YOUR GOD SAVE HER!

Dai Wan was a sixteen-year-old girl of the Pwo Karen tribe, the first patient ever to come from her village. Acutely ill, a very large spleen, fever, anemic —those are the classic signs of malaria, common there on the Thai/Burma border. But I had learned to think second and third thoughts too; the sound of hoof beats doesn't always mean horses; sometimes they are zebras or a wildebeest.

I sent a blood sample to our lab. The report soon came back, no malaria seen, but she had a very high white blood cell count, ten times the normal level. This was typical of leukemia, entirely different from malaria, and always fatal if not treated. We had a small amount of a medicine called 6-mercaptopurine, just in case we ever encountered such a patient. She improved rapidly on that, and became stronger with several blood transfusions. But as is often the case, her leukemia became resistant to it after a few weeks, and her white cell count climbed steadily higher again. No other effective medicine was available.

The Christian Sgaw Karens—a different tribal group—in Mae Sariang then suggested healing by prayer. I had no experience with it in severe cases like this, but her white cell count was back up to 76,000 and I had nothing else to offer. The church elders gathered around Dai Wan that evening and prayed with their hands resting on her head or shoulders. They prayed quite a long time.

Next morning, I did another white cell count. It was normal, about 7,000. She gained enough strength to leave the hospital. She would come back for checkups every few weeks to be sure her blood count was staying down and her spleen was still shrinking back toward normal size. She and her family took notice of the way the nurses had treated her. Her parents were very pleased, and after a few months she became a Christian, one of the first Pwo Karens from her area to do so. But a few weeks after that, her leukemia relapsed again, and her parents agreed to take her to the university hospital in Chiang Mai, 130 miles away. After several weeks of treatment there, she finally died.

Some of her relatives came from her town in the hills to attend her funeral, and they were angry. "This is what happens when you turn away from our traditional village spirits to this new religion!" they scolded the parents. "Why do you think these

Christians need a hospital next to their church!" And that's where matters stood.

It was about two years later that Dai Wan's sister appeared in church. Something about Dai Wan's attitude after she had received treatment at the hospital caused the sister to come back and find out more about the Christian way. And now, years later, many in that family and among their neighbors have become Christian.

In looking back on this, I have no scientific explanation. But I thought perhaps God might be telling the church, "See, I honor your prayers and faith, and because of that I will make her better for a time. But Dai Wan is in my care, and I have plans for her that you don't understand now."

It's easy to dismiss what happened in a foreign country as coincidence. Maybe some kind of luck gave her a normal 7,000 white cell count twelve hours after prayer.

Maybe, except that in 2003, in North Idaho, a similar event happened this time involving four cancer patients—cancer of the breast, the thyroid, the tongue, and the pancreas respectively. Each diagnosed by a medical doctor by biopsy and a pathology report, and being treated with varying success. I knew all four personally, though none were my own patients. Under the leadership of a local minister, a circle of their friends—myself among them—gathered around them one evening and prayed.

The one with advanced breast cancer died two or three months after the prayer event'

The one with pancreatic cancer lived an active life nine more years, whereas in those days almost all pancreatic cancer patients would die within six months of diagnosis. The other two are now twelve-year survivors and counting.

Often I find it best to just be thankful, even when I have no scientific answer. I cannot prove that the healing resulted from prayer or some other cause. But speaking for myself, I think prayer is the most likely explanation. More of that in the next chapter.

Sometimes Baptists argue about whether or not it's proper to cooperate with other Christian groups—Methodists, for example, or Catholics. We missionaries got along just fine with the Catholic leprosy workers in Kengtung, the Israeli doctors in the next tent at Sa Kaew refugee camp, and the Buddhist ENT surgeons and nurses who helped us at Mae Sariang one day when they cured a girl with a double cleft lip. God never expressed any objection that I am aware of. The farther we were from headquarters, the easier it seemed to be to cooperate.

Chapter 21

COINCIDENCE OR INTERVENTION?

Coincidence is not like winning the lottery. The chances of my winning it may be one in ten million or more, but someone, somewhere, does win it. It does get won. If not this week, then when the pot has grown even larger next time.

Nor does coincidence happen because someone has exerted tremendous effort to make it happen. Rather, in many cases there is no apparent reason why the outcome is what it is, but it did happen. In this physical world of cause and effect, if such events in life seem frequent, it's natural to wonder why.

Students of statistics have a number of rules to explain pure chance. If you flip a coin, the chances of it landing heads is 1 in 2. The chance of heads twice in a row is 1 in 4. Three times in a row is one in 2x2x2, (or 1 in 8) and so on. One chance in a million is 2 multipied by itself 20 times. That means that (if you have nothing better to do) flipping a perfectly balanced coin twenty times, in calm weather, no earthquakes, and no muscle fatigue, it is likely to turn

up heads all twenty times about once in a mⁱ
tries of 20 flips each, purely by chance. That is
chance predicted ahead of time. If it has already
come up heads nineteen times in a row, the chance of
heads the next time is still one in two. "Lady Luck
has no memory."

It has been said that if you give a monkey a
typewriter and allow him to pound on it at random
long enough, the laws of chance dictate that he will
eventually produce the works of William
Shakespeare. Yes, in theory it is possible, perhaps
some time in trillions of years. But probable? Don't
stand around waiting. The chance of it happening in
our human lifetime is so tiny that it might as well be
zero.

If you have witnessed some very remarkable event
in your life, it is not in itself a miracle. Considering
that seven billion people live in the world, the chance
of such an event happening somewhere to someone is
not surprising. There is a man who has been struck
by lightning three different times. Amazing? Not
necessarily; ask first if he plays golf daily, rain or
shine. If he is out in the open during thunderstorms,
he increases his lightning risk greatly.

There is a woman who won the lottery twice, but
her case does not inspire me to buy a lottery ticket.
My chance of winning this week is still about 1 in ten
million. Not a good investment strategy.

My friend and I who unexpectedly met on the
shoulder of an obscure highway in Kansas while

walking in opposite directions on a particular day? (see John Tharp's chapter) Multiple strands of coincidence came together. It would not be so remarkable if we were both scheduled to attend a board meeting in Kansas City that week. But we weren't. We hadn't met or corresponded in years.

Explaining our existence on this earth by pure chance does not seem rational to me. When coincidences of this degree happen more than two or three times in one's lifetime, one suspects that there is more than pure chance at work. And I recall at least six in my own life.

What about the "laws of nature"? Are they dependable? Experience tells us they are, to the limits of our understanding. But humans have learned a lot about nature in the past couple of centuries. Would Benjamin Franklin comprehrend atomic energy? Or a hand-held device by which one can learn news from thousands of miles away at the moment it is actually happening? Wouldn't the average person of his era consider such reports miracles (if he believed them at all)?

Are there other laws of nature we aren't yet aware of? Probably. Are they relevant to such coincidences? Who knows? Are there, for example dimensions other than length, width, height and time which will allow people to move through solids like they now do through gases and liquids? I don't know of any.

What about lying? There is always a possibility that the person telling the tale is lying, or has poor memory, or is mentally unbalanced, or was misinformed. Granting this, most of us are willing to consider the credibility of the source, and then make up our own mind.

As for the stories in this book, the same options apply. But I can vouch for the facts of each story. I was a participant, or at least a witness, in most cases. Although my short-term memory is showing the effects of aging, my long-term memory about most of these stories is reinforced by notes written soon after the event and kept in my files, and in some instances by recent interviews. I am reasonably well-educated, and have the trust of most people who know me. And I don't "do any "drugs" stronger than caffeine.

That being said, I am still confronted, like everyone, by the laws of probability and statistics, and the limits of the human mind. Do we have any evidence that our lives are affected by anything other than nature's laws and random chance? Some say we do.

Many of this world's seven billion people—perhaps most— believe in a Deity that can intervene in the world's events. Or who even created the world and all its natural laws.

Concepts of the Deity's character vary a great deal, depending on what we have been taught and on our personal experience. Even the name varies, depending on what language one speaks: God, Dieu, Allah, Yahweh, Hpaya-thakin, HprapinTsao, Gott,

Great Spirit, Dios, Shangdi, are only a few. Many people discuss the Deity's character endlessly and sometimes heatedly, as though our insistence would change that character. It seems to me wiser to try to perceive it as best we can, and behave accordingly.

Evidence for the existence of God is not accepted by everyone. There are some who accept nothing without seeing, hearing, or touching. There are some who have personal goals or desires that they consider more important. There are others who cannot fathom a God who would permit all the suffering in the world or in their own personal life, and they choose to reject the concept. Still others perhaps have never given it much thought. There are many reasons why people doubt.

The stories published here are about people who at some time have succeeded in making a favorable effect in the world. Some of them attribute the outcome to the intervention of God (by whichever name of God they are accustomed to.) When asked what makes them think God exists, they often cite any or all of three reasons:

(1) Awareness in their own life of an unusual thought or idea that did not seem connected to their mind's habitual processes. Not what we call conscience, which comes from what we've been taught. Call it imagination of what could be; call it an impulse to change life's direction, or to help someone in need. Something that in retrospect the person does not attribute to his own mind.

(2) The discovery that someone whom they trust has had similar experiences.

(3) The two-thousand-year history in written scriptures of humans seeking God (and, some will add, the history of God seeking humans.)

"Coincidence" is not synonymous with "blind chance". Coincidence only refers to events happening together. It does not address cause. A remark has been attributed to Albert Einstein: "Coincidence is God's way of remaining anonymous."

Why would God do that? I don't know; perhaps God wants to encourage us to use our minds, rather than accept a list of laws selected by people who may have an agenda of their own. I like the prophet Micah's brief summary of God's laws, "He has told you, O mortal, what is good; and what does God require of you but to do justice, love mercy, and walk humbly with your God?"

There is no way that I know of to prove God's existence or God's nature to everyone's satisfaction. In the end, each person decides for him/herself. But the decision (or lack of it) seems to have an important bearing on one's whole life.

I am aware of the idea of epiphany, where events lead to a new understanding of something – "an aha! moment" is the current popular name.

Its opposite, apophenia, is where someone sees connections where none really exist. False connections are often seen in mental illness—

schizophrenia, or in bipolar disorder, or in paranoia. It can also be seen in a war veteran with post-traumatic stress disorder (PTSD), who dives for the ground when he hears a car backfire. (Or, the war veteran may truly be more sensitive to faint warnings of danger than the rest of us are—noting the absence of people on a street maybe, or simply "bad vibes.")

Apophenia will sometimes stimulate imagination and lead to a new idea. Or, on the other hand, cause one to see something most of us would think kind of weird—an image of the Virgin Mary in a grilled cheese sandwich, for example.

All this being said, however, we are sometimes confronted with situations where the explanation "mere chance happening" is not enough to satisfy.

If such occurrences are indeed random, yet a group of them are observed together in a certain location, time, or person's life, I see three possible considerations:

(1) Faulty analysis. I am not an expert in statistics, beyond flipping a coin or watching the world population multiply. I am aware that some event that looks like one chance in a billion may actually be one chance out of thirty, after the statisticians calculate "regression to the mean," "selection," "the law of very large numbers," etc.

(2) The problem is more complicated than throwing the dice a hundred times. What I am trying to grasp are events in geography and time where the odds—in my opinion—seem extremely unlikely. It's

quite conceivable that one such event might happen in a lifetime. But several?

(3) Another way of looking at it is to consider the Universe—the whole of nature in which we live—is indeed created by a Deity. I see it as more likely than the theory of haphazard chance. The idea has been around for several thousand years, and millions of people still believe it to be true. That does not mean that we are mere pawns; we do have freedom of choice.

Since I choose to base my life behavior on one or another of these possibilities, the only choices I see (other than lying), I choose to live according to option three. Even though I can't show proof, I can choose to live as though option three is truly the best way. This is called living by faith.

The way a doubter might explore the possibility is to behave and live as if it is true, and see if it works.

"How then shall we live?"

In the Christian family in which I was brought up, the emphasis was on the two most important rules taught by Jesus: Love God. Love your neighbor. He illustrated both "love" and "neighbor" by the plight of a traveler beaten and robbed along the road and left for dead. A priest is the first to encounter him, but crosses the road to the other side and keeps going. A deacon is the next to come along the road, and he too passes by without stopping. A third traveler is a Samaritan, a group held in contempt by the upper classes of that time. He stops, treats the injured man as best he can, puts the man on the donkey he himself had been riding, and takes him to an inn; pays for a couple of days' stay, and tells the inn-keeper he'll pay any additional cost on his return trip. "Which one," Jesus asked his hearers, "treated the injured man like a neighbor?"

The story gives no reason why the first two passed on by; perhaps they have an important meeting to get to; perhaps they fear the bandits are still near by; or perhaps they just don't give a damn. We all make excuses to justify our behavior.

But to show concern for someone you don't even know requires a certain attitude in advance. Some degree of alertness to the needs of others; some degree of recognition that you yourself may someday be in need of help. Some awareness that God might help you if you ask; or offer guidance when you are uncertain.

Not an attitude like, "Being rich means never having to say you're sorry." Not, "People like that deserve what they get." Not, "My schedule is more important right now." But rather, "God, show me what to do!"

Not certain whether God is for real?

"Living by faith" often means "Try it and see." You may be surprised at the change in your life. Many have taken this route as a new beginning. The choice is yours.

BIBLIOGRAPHY

In addition to those books listed in *Bridge Ahead* (which had influenced my life and thought up to 2008), I add these more recently read works. I also read for enjoyment, but these are the ones caused me to think as well as enjoy. (F = fiction, NF = non-fiction)

Botha, Ted, *The Girl with the Crooked Nose*. New York, Random House (NF)

Brown, Daniel James, *The Boys in the Boa*t. New York, Penguin/Random, 2014 (NF)

Cronkite, Walter, *A Reporter's Life*. New York, Ballantine Books, 1997. biography (NF)

Croke. Vickie Constantine, *Elephant Company*. New York Random House, 2015 (NF)

Fadiman, Anne, *The Spirit Catches You and You Fall Down*. New York, Farrar, Straus and Giroux, 2012 (the collision of two cultures) (NF)

Forbes, Nancy and Hahon, Basil, *Faraday, Maxwell, and the Electromagnetic Field*. Amherst,

NY Prometheus Books, 2014.
how two men revolutionized physics. (NF)

Francis, Dick, *For Kicks*. Harper & Rowe, 1965 (F)

Gawande, Atul, *Being Mortal, Medicine and what matters in the end*. New York, Henry Holt, 2014 (NF)

Grisham, John, *The Street Lawyer*. New York, Doubleday 1998. The underside of Washington, (F)

Gwynne, S. C., *Empire of the Summer Moon*. New York, Scribner 2010. History of the Comanche Indian Nation (NF)

Hall, Ron and Moore, Denver, *Same Kind of Different as Me*. Nashville, TN Thomas Nelson, 2006 (NF)

Hand, David, *The Improbability Principle*. New York, Farrar, Straus and Giroux. 2014 (NF)

Holland, Travis, *The Archivist's Story*. New York, Random House, 2008. A Soviet dissident, employed to destroy books, quietly rebels (F)

Kidder, Tracy, *Home Town*. Washington Square Press, 2000 (NF)

Kidu, Carol, *A Remarkable Journey*. Sydney, Aust., Longman, 2002. Biography of the wife of the world's youngest Chief Justice (NF)

Morgan, Robert, [Daniel] *Boone*. Chapel Hill, NC, Algonquin Books, 2007. Biography (NF)

Nicolson, Adam, *God's Secretaries*. (New York, Harper Perennial, 2004) The Making of the King James Bible. History (NF)

Norton, Edward, *Death in Malaga*, An American Eyewitness Account of the Spanish Civil War (Privately published by great-nephew William Harmon, 2000) Memoirs (NF)

Penny, Louise, *How the Light Gets In*. New York, Minotore Books Canadian crime, literary (F)

Parks, Carrie Stuart, *A Cry From the Dust*. Nashville, TN, Thomas Nelson, 2014. (F)

Sendker, Jan-Philipp, *The Art of Hearing Heartbeats.* New York, Other Press (translated from German by Kevin Wiliarty © 2006)　(F)

Time [Magazine]　*Albert Einstein.* Subscriber Exclusive, 2014　biography　(NF)

ABOUT THE AUTHOR

Keith R. Dahlberg, MD is a graduate of SUNY Upstate Medical Center at Syracuse. He did three years of post-graduate internship and residency at Presbyterian Hospital of Denver, CO.

His career includes five years of solo practice in Kengtung in the East Shan State of Myanmar, a total of ten years among the hill tribes of Thailand, and a brief period with the Summer Institute of Linguistics in Papua New Guinea's East Highlands Province. In the United States, he has practiced family medicine for twenty-one years in Idaho, plus ten further years in temporary *locum tenens* work across the USA and Southeast Asia. Throughout his career, he has focused on bringing affordable medical care to the disadvantaged.

He retired from medical work at age seventy-five, and now enjoys writing. This is his seventh published book. He has served a total of twelve years on the General Board of the American Baptist Churches/USA (HQ at Valley Forge, PA).

He and his wife Lois live in Kellogg, Idaho, and are active in the ABC church in nearby Osburn, His avocational interests include geology and minerals, music, mystery novels, and humor. They have four children and nine adult grand-children.

Made in the USA
Charleston, SC
28 October 2015